Hints of Laughter, Hints of Joy

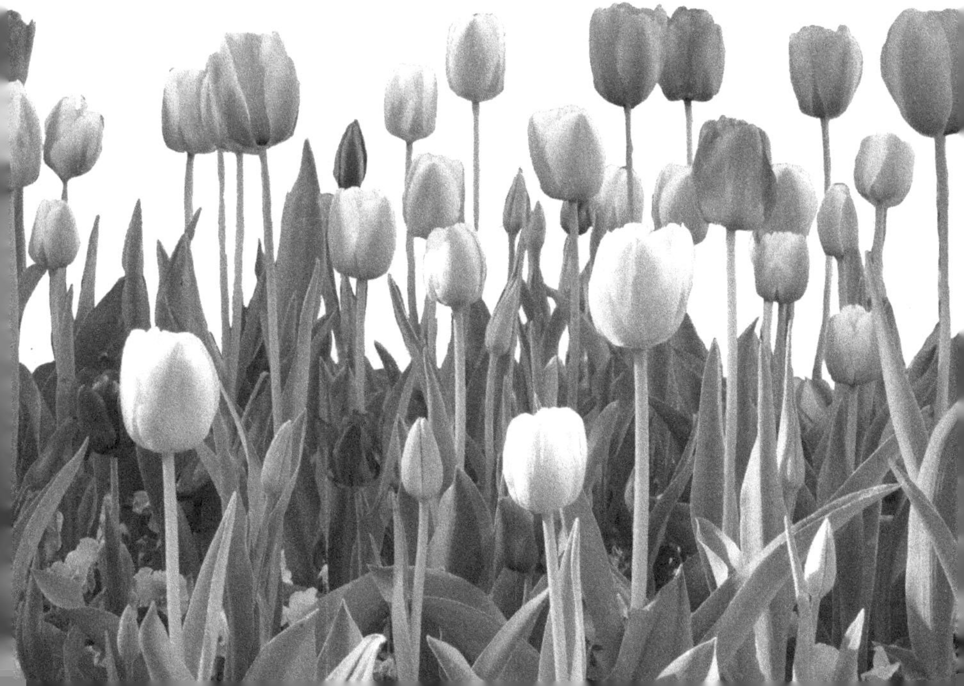

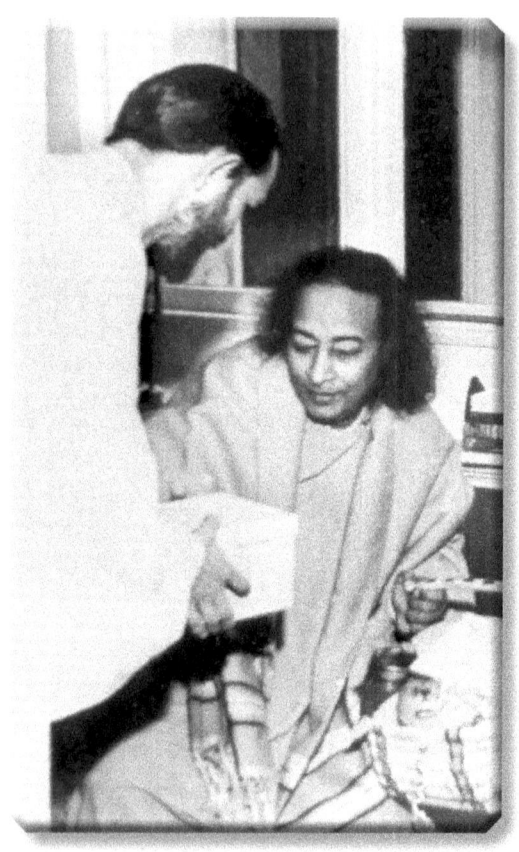

Swami Kriyananda presenting a box of *singharas* (an Indian savory) to Paramhansa Yogananda, 1952.

Hints of Laughter, Hints of Joy

The Wisdom of SWAMI KRIYANANDA, Direct Disciple of PARAMHANSA YOGANANDA

Nayaswami Padma McGilloway

CRYSTAL CLARITY PUBLISHERS Nevada City, California

© 2025 by Hansa Trust
All rights reserved. Published 2025
Printed in the United States of America

CRYSTAL CLARITY PUBLISHERS
crystalclarity.com | clarity@crystalclarity.com
14618 Tyler Foote Rd. | Nevada City, California
800.424.1055

ISBN 978-1-56589-105-0 (print) | 2024050752 (print)
ISBN 978-1-56589-518-8 (e-book) | 2024050753 (e-book)

Cover design by Tejindra Scott Tully
Interior layout and design by Michele Madhavi Molloy

The *Joy Is Within You* symbol is registered by Ananda Church of Self-Realization of Nevada County, California.

Contents

Foreword vii
Part 1: Intentional Spiritual Communities 1
    1. Community and Leadership 3
    2. Precepts for Spiritual Communities 29
    3. Community: Lessons Learned 35
    4. Practical Aspects of Community Life 49
    5. Attitudes for Living in Community 59
Part 2: Living the Inner Life 79
    6. Meditation, Concentration, and Devotion 81
    7. Satsang (Fellowship) 85
    8. Selfless Service 91
    9. Non-Attachment, Renunciation, Expansion 99
    10. Ego-Transcendence 117
    11. Intuition and Attunement 127
Afterword 163
About the Author 167
Further Explorations 169

Foreword

SWAMI KRIYANANDA WAS a direct disciple of the great master Paramhansa Yogananda, author of the spiritual classic, *Autobiography of a Yogi*. Yogananda came to America in 1920 and is well known throughout the world for his universal teachings.

Yogananda said that his teachings were not new. He did, however, describe the message he brought as a "new dispensation." Swami Kriyananda ("Swami," as we called him) always directed people's attention to Yogananda as the true guru, in much the same way that St. Francis referred people to Jesus as their savior, and not to himself.

This book offers excerpts from my own, and sometimes others', interactions with Swami. He had been empowered by his great guru to serve many seekers as a spiritual teacher; thus these accounts concern inherently spiritual matters.

Swami Kriyananda authored 150 books and more than 400 musical compositions. He lectured in many countries, in numerous languages. He founded eight spiritual communities known as Ananda, and corresponded with many thousands.

Paramhansa Yogananda told Swami as a young disciple repeatedly, "You have a great work to do." After Yogananda left his body, his chief disciple, Rajarshi Janakananda, repeated the Guru's words: "You have a great work to do—and Master will give you the strength to do it." His accomplishments, and his service, were so vast that I will not pretend to give a comprehensive account of his spiritual offerings to the world.

I did not take notes of my experiences with him at the time they occurred, though I have recounted them many times. In my forty-three years with Swami—he left his body on April 21, 2013—there were thousands of precious interactions, from which I have selected a number of jewels for this book.

Swami wrote and spoke under a number of names: James Donald Walters, J. Donald Walters, Donald Walters, Swami Kriyananda, Sri Kriyananda. I found it challenging, during the years that I was in charge of publishing his books and coordinating his lecture tours, to deal with the changes: It is harder to get traction for an author/speaker when his name keeps changing! But with hindsight I see that it helped him address the needs of different audiences, however much it made him less definable to the world.

This touches on a paradox that Swami faced throughout his life. He knew he would need to be widely known to spread Yogananda's teachings most effectively. Yet "name and fame" were at odds with his own monastic calling, and with his goal of attaining Self-realization through deep meditation and ego-transcendence.

I had the great fortune to live my life in proximity to him.

I met Swami in 1970, and in 1973 I moved to the original community he founded in Northern California. Thereafter, even during the years when we were serving in different parts of the world, and until 2013 when he left his body, we exchanged countless phone calls, emails, and notes, and I was privileged to attend many meetings where he was present, as well as teas and other informal gatherings at his home—in addition to vacations, and periods when he was a guest in our home. We often shared late-night conversations when we happened to land in the same locale. And when he was overseas, my husband and I would often get calls at midnight or after, as he knew that we were busy burning our candles at both ends! These interactions were spiritual high points in my life, during which a great deal was experienced, and much was absorbed, depending on my receptivity at the time.

I was nineteen when I met Swami. I am now seventy-three. I'm not one of those to whom writing comes easily—I much prefer a conversation. Yet when two close friends recently passed away, I realized that what I had gained from Swami (especially about leading communities) could be lost if I didn't write it down.

What I gained from my time with Swami was precious beyond words. Every moment that I was with him was a blessing on my life. In India, I once rode with him in a taxi to the airport, where he had an early flight. It was 3 a.m., in fact, and we were quiet as the driver made his way through the typical chaotic Indian traffic.

Suddenly Swami asked me, "Why did you come on this drive to the airport?" I replied, "For the blessing." Every moment in his presence was a moment when I felt closer to God.

Yet, although it may seem paradoxical, we were less likely to find ourselves in his presence if we viewed him personally. The more *impersonally* we related to him, the more he could freely enjoy our friendship together. Through the subtle guidance he offered, I learned to perceive the *"Hints of Laughter, Hints of Joy"* that permeated my life.

I realize that further explanation is in order. One of my favorite songs of Swami's is "God's Call Within." It begins:

Listen! Listen!
Whispering within your soul:
Hints of laughter, hints of joy;
Sweet songs of sadness, of quenchless yearning
For the Light,
For My love, your true home.

Viewed through the lens of this song, this book will capture a fraction of these hints of laughter and of joy that I experienced in my years with Swami. There are hundreds more, but included in these pages are those that I hope may be most helpful to others. These hints are universal. The Divine resides at the heart of every atom in creation, and we are all woven from those lustrous threads.

In the early days of the community, on the Friday night at the end of the annual Spiritual Renewal Week, Swami would tell stories of his days with Paramhansa Yogananda. It was held in summer, mostly outdoors in nature, under a large tree next to the first temple, under a starlit sky. On one occasion, Swami told us that the stories of his time with Yogananda came most naturally and easily to mind when he needed them to support a spiritual point in a talk. What I experienced in writing this book is that once I wrote a few of these recollections, they came pouring through, filling the pages. I see this as a special dispensation to share them with future generations of truth seekers.

PART 1

Intentional Spiritual Communities

Paramhansa Yogananda said that someday intentional spiritual communities would spread "like wildfire."

Here, I will record my memories of many things that Swami said or did. I believe that if spiritual communities in general, and the communities he founded specifically, spread into the future, then those residing in, and especially those leading these communities might find his counsel as invaluable as I did.

If you have not already read it, I heartily recommend Swami's book, *The Need for Spiritual Communities, and How to Start Them*. It offers a fascinating account, based on his fifty years creating and leading communities, of the principles that he saw as essential for their success.

Swami knew that the communities of the future would not be able to depend on him as the founder. With the right spirit, they would expand into the future because they are based on simple spiritual principles. Swami attuned himself to Yogananda's vision for communities, and in founding eight successful communities himself, he was able to demonstrate the validity of the high precepts upon which their success was based.

When I arrived at the first community that Swami founded, I was nineteen years old. I was not drawn to the communitarian aspects of life there; I was drawn to Swami—the man who was a direct disciple of Yogananda, and who emanated such a deep, palpable peace, joy, and calmness. It was those qualities that I wanted to develop myself. I looked around at the other residents and saw a small group of rag-tag devotees that I wasn't so sure about.

In time, the community aspect too became extremely important to me, as I realized how wonderfully freeing it was to live among like-minded people who shared my high aspirations. Community living also supports a life of ego-transcendence, much as rocks in a rock tumbler become beautiful and smooth! Many of those seemingly ragtag devotees became my closest friends.

Chapter One

Community and Leadership

When the community was still small, the leadership was not yet clearly defined. As in any group of people, those with good spirit were looked upon with respect, and often deferred to for important decisions. But once the community had grown to a point where it was no longer possible to manage it in that way, Swami called several of us together to brainstorm a system of governance for the communities as they moved into the future.

At the meeting, Swami posed a question: What would be an ideal form of leadership for a spiritual community? He brought up, as an example, the American system of checks and balances that was meant to keep the three branches of government—legislative, executive, judicial—in a state of balance, harmony, and cooperation.

Swami offered the example as a starting point for further discussion, though not necessarily as something to be duplicated. We left the meeting with an assignment to meditate on these thoughts, and to return the following day with insights for a workable system.

At the next meeting, after some initial discussion, Swami proposed an idea: Each community would have a spiritual director and a general manager. The spiritual director would look out for the spiritual welfare of the individuals, and the general manager would concern himself with the welfare of the community as a whole.

In this way, a system of checks and balances would be appropriate also for communities such as ours. The spiritual director and general manager would work in close cooperation.

It seemed a brilliant solution, and it has worked beautifully not only at that original community, but also, since 1986, in the other spiritual communities Swami founded around the world. I imagine that in a more enlightened age, the two roles could be merged, as issues requiring checks and balances would be resolved easily by an enlightened leader. But for now, the system has served us well.

Just as a community's geographical terrain and climate can influence its character—think of remote villages high in the Himalayas, or cities in the desert—so too will the community's character naturally be influenced by the character of its leader. A community, for example, whose leader had exceptional artistic talents might generate income not from businesses but through art and musical productions.

Another type of leader might be skilled at offering educational programs, or practical services to serve the interests of the wider local area. One community might have a strong interest in dramatic performances, while another might focus on creating organic gardens and orchards. Each community will be flavored to a large degree by the talents and interests of its leaders.

❧

Another principle that Swami stressed is that a position of leadership does not indicate that the leader knows everything that needs knowing. Others can supply the necessary know-how; indeed, a good leader can often attract them. Sometimes, and more likely so in a spiritual community, a leader may receive his position in part in order to learn the lessons that the position can teach him, including, of course, lessons in the art of leadership itself.

Swami, like Yogananda, said that the highest qualification of a successful leader is the desire to serve. Anyone wishing, on the other hand, to appear all-knowing, or to bask in others' attention, will be ill-suited to a leadership position.

❧

Years ago, the community where I lived at the time, in Seattle, Washington, received a large donation to build a beautiful temple. The temple was designed by a Swiss architect, and modeled after a similar structure near Assisi, Italy.

Building the temple was a massive undertaking for a community of our size. Between raising the funds (including a mortgage) and construction, it took a little over seven years. When the temple was finally completed, I was thrilled to tell Swami that its doors would open as soon as he could come to bless it!

He responded, "You see—I didn't have to be directly involved. You all were able to accomplish this." I understood his meaning.

Swami taught us, including by words and his example, that a leader should delegate whenever possible. In this way, many people can receive the blessing of allowing the Divine to flow through them. Moreover, he didn't merely delegate: He gave constant inner support and guidance.

༺༻

Grassroots decision-making normally means that those most directly involved with a project are empowered to make decisions regarding it, and allowed to move it forward without seeking constant permission. Centralized decision-making, by contrast, means that every decision must be run through the overall leadership, even if the leaders are living at a great distance, in another community, nation, or even on another continent.

A good leader will encourage grassroots decision-making by first ensuring that there is a competent leader at the local level. He will then step out of the way and allow the person in charge locally to make the decisions (and mistakes). Swami was such a leader. Grassroots decision-making seemed risky at times, but it somehow always worked out for the best.

༺༻

Swami encouraged decentralization—which is another way of saying that he advocated grassroots decision-making. In a booklet that he published in the early 1970s on intentional spiritual communities, he advocated a model in which communities would be legally and financially autonomous, though bound together in the most important way: spiritually.

It would take fifty years for the communities that Swami founded to achieve a fully decentralized structure. Today they are flourishing, united by a common spiritual aspiration, though scattered across the globe.

Most organizations, it seems, have an unfortunate tendency to attract leaders who love to be in control. Any ego-born desire to control others, however, is an impediment, not only to the leader's ability to serve the organization and its members, but to his own spiritual welfare. Thus Swami worked hard to ensure that the communities would be organized in a manner that would help and not hinder the spiritual welfare of all of us, including the leaders.

❧

"A work often dies with its founder." This common fate motivated Swami's strong effort to select and train good-spirited leaders. He wanted the communities to be able to move forward in the right spiritual and practical directions without his constant outward presence. Thus, he trained the leaders to go directly to the ultimate Source for their guidance. And, drawing on that guidance, to support others by praying for them and their needs, by involving them, by giving them responsibility, and by checking in lightly to support them as needed.

Swami was a superb leader because he spoke and acted only as God guided him inwardly. For those of us who witnessed the unfailing wisdom behind his decision-making, it was tempting to leave the last word to him, and thus avoid the risks in making decisions ourselves. For this reason, to help us grow as leaders, for some of us it was best to live at a distance from Swami, so that we could be thrown in at the deep end and learn to swim. If he had hovered in the background, it would have been a constant temptation to seek his explicit guidance.

This was something I experienced many times, when Swami put me in charge of large projects without expressing clear expectations. Swami was always concerned about our growth—he would give us all the freedom we needed to learn from our successes and mistakes. Being put in charge without detailed instructions forced me to reach deep for inner, intuitive guidance. It was only when I didn't get it right that he might give a gentle hint to point me back in the right direction. In this way, he helped me grow at my own pace.

Paramhansa Yogananda lived and taught intuitively; he rarely spelled out what he intended. Swami, too, taught and led intuitively. If he asked you to do a job, he would always offer it as a choice; it was never a command. Nor would he define the task in detail. Thus we had to go inside to find the right guidance. Thus we learned to live intuitively.

I was sitting with Swami one day when he decided to telephone one of the departments for some information. When one of the co-managers answered, he asked to speak to the other manager. Once he had the information, he put down the phone and said, "I didn't want the first co-manager to think he was in charge. I wanted him to understand that even though they are co-managers, it is really his partner who is in charge."

Swami's guidance to us was nuanced and subtle; it took account of factors that most of us were often unable to perceive. We had to listen carefully to understand his meaning.

❦

Swami didn't "mentor" us. Rather, he threw us in beyond our depth, but then unfailingly supported and guided us: with counsel as needed, or through our own intuition—as we swam to shore.

❦

Swami said, "I'm not the type of person who puts my arm around your shoulder and says in a quavering voice, 'Now Johnny. . . .'" He was telling us that he wouldn't comfort us in our delusions, simply to try to make us feel better.

Swami was always compassionate. Sometimes his compassion would be expressed in words, though more often it was a vibration of love and support. But it was never emotional.

I will share some leadership principles that Swami consistently emphasized:

❧

Make decisions based on what is the right thing to do, rather than on finances or what the world might think.

❧

In group dynamics, when there's a need to share important news, do so first with those most directly involved; then with those indirectly involved; and finally with those with no involvement (usually the largest group). Whenever possible, include the first groups in the larger meeting.

❧

When the first community was very young and the life there was still quite rustic, Swami felt it was time to start a community in San Francisco. Somehow, we were able to locate and lease a large mansion in the exclusive neighborhood of Pacific Heights. It had forty-four rooms and cost $4,500 per month to lease.

Swami led by example. He knew that for most of the residents of our rural community, it would be a huge leap to consider moving to luxurious quarters in the San Francisco ashram. And so he began by taking a room in the mansion himself. Only then did he hold a meeting of the residents and extend the invitation: "Who will join me?"

About twenty Ananda Village people plus twenty San Francisco devotees immediately committed to participate in the adventure and move into the new ashram. The location served us well for many years, until we decided to move the main Bay Area center to Palo Alto, fifty miles south.

❦

Of course, a leader cannot be expected to lead by example and also direct, much less perform, all the tasks of a community. There simply aren't enough hours in a day. In relevant situations, Swami would sometimes remark that if the leader took care of all the details, the project might never be completed. He was concerned, above all, that the spirit be right: expansive, positive, in service to the Divine. He said that he never left the leaders on their own, but that his support and guidance were always with them. He was concerned to ensure that *their* spirit and support, in turn, were felt in all the arenas where they asked others to serve.

❦

"Roll up your sleeves and get your hands dirty." I heard Swami say this to someone who had misunderstood the principle of delegating and had become a passive "armchair manager." When Swami delegated the responsibility for a project, he would actively engage with the person, by calling or meeting with him to ask questions and offer his input and support as needed.

It was by tuning in to Swami's example that I learned to delegate. I realized that the best way to delegate responsibility to others is first to involve them in the project and see if their interest is enthusiastic enough to let them take charge. Not everyone will be keen, but if we make a habit of involving others, we will soon find the people who will enjoy taking it on.

I used to worry that if I delegated too much, I wouldn't have anything to do! Of course, I was gravely mistaken. Allowing others to take on some of our tasks frees us to take on new and more interesting projects. I realized that this is the divine law, and that once we've delegated a task, it's important to give the person as much responsibility as possible, and then give him a wide berth.

There was a person in the community who said that he had lots of management and retail experience. When he ran a business in the community, and it began to lose significant amounts of money, Swami invited him to run a business that was five times larger than the first! Of course, some of us were trembling at the thought of what might happen. But he soon declined the larger project and moved away.

I realized that Swami's kind gesture had given him not only the spiritual support he needed, but also the confidence to move on with his life. At the time, Swami's offer seemed risky, but spiritually it was absolutely right for this person. A leader may need to make decisions for the good of the individual, rather than the project itself.

❧

Hold the reins of leadership loosely. Share the responsibility with as many as will accept it in the right spirit.

❧

In making decisions, large and small, Swami always sought to involve others. He never assumed that the right answers were preordained. Instead, he carefully considered others' input, and the outcome was often a surprise.

As an example, when we left the mansion in San Francisco to form a community in Palo Alto, California, it was situated in a large rented ramshackle summer home in the wealthy suburb of Atherton. The leaders knew that it was only a foothold: temporary quarters while we explored the possibility of purchasing an apartment complex to house the community.

The main community in the Sierra foothills was situated then on approximately eight hundred acres, which were community owned. The apartment complex near Palo Alto would be far too expensive for us to purchase outright; it would have to be owned by a group of residents and friendly investors. When Swami first learned of the idea, he expressed doubts.

At the time, my husband and I ran the finances of the main community, and we, too, had our doubts. Swami asked the Palo Alto leaders and some of the leaders at the main community to come together and discuss the matter.

At that meeting, the Palo Alto leaders made a convincing case for the model they were advocating and explained why it was the best option for a community in a large city. Swami immediately embraced the concept and supported the project. The community, located in Mountain View, California, next to Palo Alto, continues to operate on the same ownership basis today.

My husband and I, too, learned from direct experience, when we were later asked to direct the Seattle community, the suitability of this model to urban communities. It allowed us to grow, and so to offer greater numbers of newer people the benefits of living in community. In the case of the Seattle community, the ownership structure is an LLC, and the management is local and onsite, which gives the community autonomy.

Swami was able to see the outcome of an action or a project far into the future. But unless the outcome would be harmful to an individual or to the community, he would give people freedom to learn from their mistakes.

❧

Patience in leadership was a quality that Swami tirelessly demonstrated, and that he advised others to practice. I remember being in a group with him as we looked at a map of the first community. When someone pointed to an area marked "Cluster C," Swami said, "Oh yes, that's where I had hoped we would build the school."

This was years after a school had been built in the middle of the community (far away from Cluster C, which was at the edge of the property). At the time, Swami had explained that some children might not have chosen to live in a spiritual community, even though their parents had. They might have very different karma, and having the school on a separate parcel of land, away from the center of the community, would allow them to feel freer to follow their own interests. Otherwise, it could have a negative impact on the community's spiritual focus, especially during the willful teenage years.

Roughly ten years after Swami shared this thought, the needs of the teenage students did, in fact, begin to impact the community's spiritual life. It took time and much painstaking effort before a balance could be found, where several adults who were skilled at working with teenagers were able to guide their activities in positive directions without stifling their energy and their budding need to flex their will power and independence. Had the school been situated farther from the community's "downtown," it is likely that this troublesome phase could have been avoided.

❧

A follower of another path loved to come to our temple. When his guru came to Seattle, this person invited us to come and meet him. We didn't want to insult him or hurt his feelings, yet we weren't interested in going. The next time Swami called, we asked for his advice. Without skipping a beat, he suggested that we accept the man's invitation, and when we met the guru, to tell him that he, Swami Kriyananda, also extended greetings. In this simple way, he showed us how to handle a delicate situation while remaining true to our path.

❧

I once asked Swami what I should do if I met a new person about whom I had an intuition he would eventually stab us—our community—in the back. He responded that we should serve him anyway. In other words, we should serve everyone who comes, without concern for what he might do to us, or for us.

❧

When the leader of the Portland community found a large building for sale at a reasonable price, Swami was thrilled at the prospect of our being able to live and serve together in one place. Such a property could possibly become our headquarters.

He invited my husband and me and two others to fly with him from Grass Valley, California, to Portland in a small rented plane to save time and, to our surprise, also money. When we arrived, we walked around the building, which was massive, and had been built as a mental hospital.

At the end of the viewing, Swami asked us to share our thoughts about the place, reserving his own thoughts for last. He wanted us to dig deep and express our own impressions. After we had all spoken, he explained that because the building was designed to be an institution, its vibrations felt overwhelmingly heavy and rigid. He said that the vibration of the building would be impossible to overcome, and would influence us in ways that would not be helpful for an expansive work such as ours. He took the opportunity to open our eyes to the impact that architecture has on our consciousness.

In general, it's the people that make a community—not the buildings. But the vibration of a building can influence people positively or negatively. And so we should try to find, or build, structures that emit, or invite, a higher consciousness. Such buildings will have three main characteristics, which Swami incorporated in the title of a book he wrote about the construction of his home, Crystal Hermitage, that he'd had built to his own design: *Space, Light, and Harmony.*

Swami urged the community to keep those guidelines—space, light, and harmony—in mind when acquiring or constructing our homes, temples, and workplaces. He had long been intrigued by the geodesic domes conceived by Buckminster Fuller, and admired Fuller's genius in architecture. He felt that the dome energetically enhanced the practice of meditation because it was similar to the shape of the human head. Furthermore, in the Indian system of the *yugas* (cycles of time), the circle or dome is the shape of a future, more enlightened age. His original home, as well as several other buildings in the community, were geodesic domes.

After he had lived for several years in Europe, Swami returned to the community and received a tour of the new homes that had been built during his absence. They were all rectangular. At the end of the tour, Swami expressed modest disappointment at the lack of geodesic domes. Later, he explained that, in contrast to our community, some of the most attractive villages in Europe had a certain cohesion in their architecture that reflected coordination and harmony among the inhabitants.

He also realized, however, that families struggled with the single large, open space inside a dome. Even if walls were constructed inside, they could not extend up to the ceiling; the noise of children at play was therefore an issue. Swami let go of the ideal of the dome, but he urged us to create a committee to review peoples' architectural plans, so as to ensure some semblance of harmony in the community's overall design.

❧

Always be willing to question your first principles. This was a guideline that Swami emphasized again and again. It is important to behave consciously, and not simply accept a teaching or new idea blindly. Study it—does it make sense? Do you resonate with it? Will it work? This is the scientific approach to spirituality. It applies doubly for leadership in a community. In order to lead effectively, we must be able to accept other points of view, and be willing to reevaluate our own position and decisions.

❧

We cannot pour new wine into old wineskins. Start fresh! I had the great blessing to lead a new department that Swami had created. His reason for doing so had been to bring in fresh, creative thinking to replace the traditional advice and limitations that he was being offered at the time. Instead of arguing with the people who didn't agree with him, he avoided a confrontation by simply starting a new department.

❧

When Swami published a book for parents and teachers called *Education for Life*, some people suggested that we bring its fresh concepts into the public schools by offering to train the teachers. Swami explained that it would be extremely difficult to get a system with a longtime momentum behind it to change direction. We would have greater success, he said, if we started our own schools based on the system. Once those schools were successful, other educators would of their own accord take notice and want to learn the system.

※

Swami used to test the validity of an intuition he'd received by presenting it to the community, and observing from their responses whether it was helpful or not.

※

I recall a talk that Swami gave in the early years of the first community he founded, to about sixty people. It took place outdoors in the shade of a lovely tree. In the midst of the talk, a man I didn't recognize stood up to the side and near the back of the group and began taking off his clothes! His expression seemed mentally unbalanced.

Two of our stronger male residents immediately walked over and picked up his clothes, covered him in a meditation shawl, and gently guided him away. When I looked back at Swami, he was his usual calm, unperturbed self. He continued his talk without even a slight pause, as his calmness continued to hold us in an aura of peace. Sometimes, leadership means guiding others by our example, without words.

The first location of Swami's community in Italy was a large summer villa near Lake Como that a friend had loaned to us. It was beautiful in summer, and it afforded the guests an ideal and peaceful environment for spiritual retreat. As summer gave way to fall, however, we came to realize that the term "summer villa" indeed meant literally that: a villa for the summer months only! It soon grew so cold inside that the staff would work and hold meetings covered head to toe by down blankets.

When my husband and I visited the next fall, we listened to many war stories about the cold. Sitting near Swami at lunch, I heard him talking with the owner of the villa, and suggesting that we build another structure in front that would be insulated and have affordable heating.

When I saw Swami later that day, I said something implying it was a good strategy, because she would be so overwhelmed with the thought of constructing another villa that she would agree to install a better heating system in the existing one. Swami turned to me and said, "I didn't make the suggestion to have that result. I simply felt the inspiration from Divine Mother to offer it."

Accustomed as we are to the ways of this world, it is all too easy to assume that everyone has a "strategy." I learned from Swami again and again that his only "strategy" was to live in the moment, in attunement with the Divine. True leadership is following one's intuitive guidance.

In running a spiritual community, Swami often thought of the people who would come later, and who hadn't yet found us. He devised ways to leave a trail of "breadcrumbs" to help them find their way home. In the early days, he offered monthly inspirational pamphlets. At least twice, he recorded a full year of brief daily radio shows. Later, he created a television series for every day of the year. Leadership isn't only serving those present, but extending help to those who *might* come.

Swami encouraged us to start all kinds of businesses, and to exercise our creativity in developing ways to earn an income through community-owned or private enterprises, and in this way to strengthen the community's ability to serve and to gain financial stability.

For communities to include families, there will have to be jobs to support them. Swami often told us that he hoped we would someday have a department for each of his 150 books, so that members could earn an income while serving the spiritual needs of people throughout the world. "You must be practical in your idealism," Yogananda told Swami. By extension, spiritual communities require "practical idealism" in order to thrive.

Swami asked me to lead an independent department that would act on his guidance in implementing the inspirations he felt from God. He said that it was the job of the community leaders to look out for the welfare of the entire community, and by separating himself from those responsibilities he could feel free to follow God's guidance in writing, music, tours, and more, knowing that the community was in safe hands.

Leaders need to balance considerations of immediate welfare and the call of forward-moving inspiration. An example that comes to mind is President Kennedy's support of the space program.

※

The beautiful design of the Blue Lotus Temple in Bothell, Washington, with its curved, blue-tiled roof and lighted cupola, was modeled after the original Temple of Light in Assisi, Italy. When we began planning its construction, we held a large fundraising event, where I presented some of the ways in which we could reach the amount needed to complete the project.

Swami spoke after me, saying: "Padma just showed you how we can raise enough to build the temple. In Assisi, however, they didn't know how much it would cost, and yet they built it anyway."

Swami was reminding us that if a thing is right to do, we should tackle it even if at first we can't see how we'll succeed. If it is the right thing, Divine Mother will help us. Not only did She help us build the temple: Fourteen years later in 2020, in the midst of a pandemic, She helped us again. At that time, we mounted a campaign to pay off the entire mortgage. We raised $1.3 million in less than three months! When we act for the right, Divine Mother will indeed lend Her support.

※

Swami would often warn against letting mundane financial and legal considerations influence us excessively. This was especially important, he said, for the leaders. Swami cited examples of great spiritual teachers whose organizations came to concern themselves too much with "practical matters"—most famously among them, certain followers of St. Francis who became obsessed with the importance of organizing and spreading his teachings.

※

Swami placed great importance on the role of the arts in a spiritual community. Eventually he created an annual Festival of the Joyful Arts, inviting artists to display and perform the art they had developed based on their spiritual inspiration. These festivals attracted many hundreds of souls over the three years they took place. They were discontinued at that point due to scheduling conflicts, but I expect this is one of the many seeds Swami sowed that will bear more fruit in later years.

Because the arts often don't produce much income, Swami urged us to find ways to support the artists in the community. Among his suggestions: purchasing their art to display in our public buildings, holding concerts and theatrical productions, and paying royalties for the writing of books. In the early days, when we were always stretched financially, this was not easy to do. Yet, even at that time, he strongly encouraged the leaders to make it a priority.

❧

They say that when Paramhansa Yogananda was alive it was almost impossible to organize the work, as he would regularly throw "spanners into the works."

It was similar with Swami. I would no sooner obtain a measure of success by following his guidance than he would change directions—often even multiple times in one day! For example, he once asked our department to work on a book-promotion plan that would require the full-time effort of everyone on our small staff. Then, moments later, he called again and asked two of the staff to help him with his upcoming speaking tour. He then met with yet another staff member and asked him to look into moving our entire operation to the San Francisco Bay Area. At the end of days like that one, I felt fairly dizzy!

Later, I would finally be blessed with the understanding that what seemed to be happening on the outside was never what was actually happening; the spiritual life is within us, and the inner life is ultimately all that matters.

He could have articulated this teaching (in fact he often did), but I would never have understood the lesson as clearly without *experiencing* his amazing willingness to risk failure by making so many conflicting requests, if it would help us be more in tune with the guidance of Spirit within. The beauty of this way of teaching was that he never stirred the pot for motives of his own; he was simply following divine guidance.

Toward the end of his life, Swami encouraged all the city communities to buy land in the countryside nearby, as a safe haven for troubled times. When Yogananda started a school in Ranchi, India, he had the young boys do lots of gardening, because he felt that it was both a spiritually nurturing activity and something that would prove helpful if the need arose.

Because most of the communities didn't have funds to buy land, the purchases were organized by groups of member investors, who added their funds to any that were available in the community.

The rural properties have been developed as farms and retreats, the details depending on the skills of the community's members. Swami often repeated Yogananda's predictions about troubled times ahead. He hoped that in times of need these properties would enable us to stay safe and be of help to others.

When Swami asked me to manage his special projects, the department was called the Joyful Arts Production Association. Its offices were in a small building with four tiny rooms, no indoor plumbing, and just one telephone with a very long cord that we could carry from room to room. Our staff was small. The only products were a set of audio cassettes of Swami reading the stories of P. G. Wodehouse, a famous British writer of humorous books, and a few cassette recordings of his songs. I had no idea how we could begin to support even such a tiny staff.

When I met with Swami, I asked him, "What is the Joyful Arts Production Association?" He replied, "It's that part of the community which goes out."

I went back to my office, even more perplexed. "Go out with what?" I wondered. And, "Who will go out?"

The next day, when I saw him again, the same exchange transpired. Again, he replied that it was the part of the community that would "go out." And once more, I left thoroughly perplexed.

However, after thinking about it, I arranged a concert of music under the stars, featuring the singers and also Swami. At the end of the evening, I counted the income (the first real income so far!)—whereupon Swami promptly scooped it up to pay the Crystal Hermitage expenses!

When I organized another evening under the stars, the result was the same. Thus, I was forced to consider that this might not be fulfilling my mandate to "go out." Although the events were successful, they produced no income for the new department. I knew that I would have to dig deep for inspiration and, above all, guidance.

Over the next two years, Swami began writing books again, and I learned to publish them. Then came traveling to the publishing trade shows to sell them and find distributors, plus organizing of sales teams to go out on the road to sell the books to bookstores, while simultaneously arranging to give talks in the stores, or at New Thought churches.

At about this time, Swami composed an exquisite oratorio called *Christ Lives!*, which we recorded and helped him coordinate with color slides he'd taken of the Holy Land. Before long, we were able to book the Oratorio program into churches around the country.

With little time even to think about it, we were suddenly launched and "going out." My experience illustrates the way in which he led. He would never sit us down and spell things out in detail. Instead, he taught us to commune inwardly and use our own intuition. Though this way may be slower, the spiritual benefits were immense, and the fruits were refreshing beyond the power of imagination.

Chapter Two

Precepts for Spiritual Communities

"Don't make too many rules—they kill the spirit."
—PARAMHANSA YOGANANDA

W<small>E LIVE IN</small> a time when governments enact so many laws, and addenda to the laws, that it requires highly specialized attorneys to help us find our way through the weeds.

Too often in our society, order is established by making rules, and more rules. But overreliance on rules can make us inflexible. The spiritual life works with intuition, which is fluid. Add to this that each person's spiritual journey is unique, and it becomes essential to avoid making rules whenever possible! Hence Yogananda's counsel to the monastics: *Too many rules kill the spirit.*

The communities founded by Swami Kriyananda have only two main rules: no drugs, and no alcohol. Everything else is sorted out on a case-by-case basis. It's a refreshing and important feature of the communities: It encourages flexibility, and allows us to seek creative solutions appropriate to the individual.

People are more important than things. Swami's guidance was always closely aligned with this principle. He explained: "People, especially in their spiritual needs, will always be more important than any organizational exigency. This statement must, however, be construed in the light of divine truth, which, although always loving, is at the same time impersonal. Thus, even as physicians may demonstrate greater actual compassion when they inflict a temporary pain on their patients than when they spare them the pain but ensure a much greater suffering later, the rule of divine compassion is sometimes stern, necessarily so, and may not be immediately appreciated by its recipients."

❧

The community members were asked to take on certain jobs or responsibilities, and even to relocate to help out in another community. But they were always free to make their own decisions, and sometimes people would decline a job or a move. Even if the community's need was great, the freedom of the individual to choose was an important principle, because *people are more important than things.*

❧

At other times, when a decision or outcome wasn't to someone's liking, he might cry, "People are more important than things!"—when what he was really saying was that his desires weren't being considered. These were the cases that Swami was referring to when he said, "The rule of divine compassion is sometimes stern, necessarily so, and may not be immediately appreciated by its recipients." In a spiritual community, there are countless opportunities to test this teaching. Learning when it applies and when it doesn't requires intuition, experience, and awareness that our ego-attached desires will always try to cloud our discernment.

❧

Jato dharma, tato jaya: Where there is adherence to right attitude and action, there is victory. Indeed, a community should define victory itself in terms of this principle, and never seek victory, even for the sake of its own survival, at the cost of this principle. If a community's institutional survival demands that this ideal be compromised, survival itself will no longer be worthwhile. For a spiritual community is primarily a *spiritual* ideal.

Swami often cited an example that occurred after the forest fire that destroyed much of the first community. Some neighbors' homes and land were also devastated by the fire, and they decided to sue the county: It had been determined that a faulty spark arrestor on a county truck had started the fire, and they won millions. But Swami decided that we wouldn't sue. Instead, he wrote to the county officials, telling them that we would not be suing: that we did not wish to take our bad luck out on our neighbors.

❧

See if it works! The ultimate test of any idea, in a spiritual community or anywhere else, is whether it *actually works*. We must approach the spiritual life in the spirit of a scientist—and find out for ourselves if a teaching delivers on its promises. Our spirituality must be tested in the cold light of day, as Yogananda's foremost woman disciple used to say. In spiritual communities especially, perhaps, it would be too easy to live in the realm of ideas. Ideas must be grounded and made manifest.

❧

Countless times through the years, Swami said: *"If the spirit is right, everything will turn out as it should."* Sometimes we were in the middle of a severe test. Other times he might ask a person who seemed unqualified to take a position of responsibility. It was difficult to see how he could succeed at the task. And yet Swami would say, "He has good spirit. It will be fine." Outwardly things might not have looked fine, but I came to understand that this had little to do with the underlying realities that Swami could see. Things did, in fact, turn out for the best if the spirit was right, because people grew spiritually in the process; or because kindness won the day.

❧

Do it now! Swami learned this precept early in his years with Yogananda. Yogananda urged all those in training with him to complete tasks quickly and efficiently. This forced an attitude essential in the spiritual life: the "attitude" of high energy.

※

Swami lived to be eighty-six, and his days were filled with work for God: founding 8 communities, writing 150 books, composing more than 400 musical compositions, and giving thousands of lectures and talks in several languages. He told us that his accomplishments were possible because he adhered to the dictum "Do it now!" He lived in the moment. He completed a task to which he had committed himself, letting nothing stand in the way, and then he would plunge into the next.

An example was his launching of new communities in India when he was seventy-seven years old, even though his health was extremely precarious. After settling in India, he realized that television would be a wonderful way to reach millions. And so he filmed 10 episodes per day in order to make the 365 needed for the year. As I watched him record one twenty-minute program after another, often all day, I was squirming in my seat, visualizing a comfortable bed, while he expounded fresh wisdom hour after hour.

※

Swami joined us for an event to raise money for our community in Washington. A large poster showed the original community, which was forty-five years old, and the Washington community, which was twenty-five. Swami leaned over to me and said, "All of our communities were born in 1920, when Yogananda came to America!" *Honor your roots.*

Chapter Three

Community: Lessons Learned

WHEN SWAMI INVITED me to manage his special projects, the community's publishing department told him that his latest book would cost about $40,000 to publish. Swami knew that he would write many books, but at such a high cost they would never be published. He had learned of a new technology called desktop publishing. (It was 1985, in the fledgling days of personal computers.) The equipment cost about $10,000, but if someone in the community could run it, we would save tens or even hundreds of thousands of dollars over time.

The trouble was that the quality of the books was inferior to books printed on a real press. The publishing world looked upon those books as inferior, and distributors were less likely to take them on. Nevertheless, it would open a path for dozens of books to pour through him to help people.

The lesson was: Don't wait for perfection. Take whatever steps you must to move forward in the right *direction,* and let God guide you from there.

In Swami's case it was not about selling books; it was about the ability to share the life-changing *ideas* they contained. He didn't want the years to slip away without their being published:

They were too important for us to defer to someone else's quality standard.

Crystal Clarity Publishers has become very successful. Partly it owes its success to the staff's deep attunement to the material they publish. Their loving dedication has propelled the books into unexpected markets and opened many opportunities. As director of Foreign Rights to this day, I've seen their popularity spread far abroad, as foreign publishers have made them available in more than fifty languages. Swami always felt that lasting success in any business comes through individual, caring relationships and continuity of personnel. I myself have been working with aspects of the community's publishing for more than forty years.

❧

At a certain point, the first community Swami founded had grown quite large. It was situated on over 800 acres and had a population of about 250 adults and 80 children. The local government kept making the requirements for building new homes ever more difficult to meet. When the process became intolerable, Swami consulted a community resident who was an attorney. She researched the possibility of the community's becoming its own incorporated city, and found that we met the legal requirements. As a "city," however small, we could adopt more reasonable building requirements. We applied to the county for the necessary permission.

To make a—very—long story short, over the next many months we fought a creative battle with great effort against neighbors who distrusted our motives and opposed the plan. Just as this drama approached its climax, Swami contacted the team and said that he had come to see that incorporating as a town would not be a wise step for a spiritual community. He explained that it would require too much emphasis on the secular functions of running a town, while taking away from our time to live a spiritual life.

Despite our considerable momentum at that point—and the public embarrassment that ensued when we changed our position—we turned on a dime and dropped our efforts to incorporate.

A person with a difficult personality applied for community membership. The membership committee members were reluctant to accept her, knowing that she would be a source of trouble. When Swami learned of the proposed decision, he advised that if we didn't accept her, we would have to go out and find someone just like her. In a spiritual community, the members aspire to grow spiritually, which means that we seek to overcome our limitations. It is precisely the people who test us who are best able to help us become spiritually mature.

The community's guest retreat was urgently in need of more guest rooms. Of course, there weren't funds to build them. We asked an artist to make a sketch of the proposed dormitory. We placed it on a large fundraising poster that we mounted near the dining area, where the guests would see it. After a year, not one dollar had been donated for the dormitory.

Swami then suggested that instead of building a single large dormitory, perhaps we should raise funds for several smaller buildings. We duly removed the sign and initiated a campaign for smaller buildings that would be more affordable and could be built one at a time. This generated the right energy. Where there had been little enthusiasm for the dormitory concept, donations began to come in, and soon we were breaking ground for the first simple guest house. The lesson: *Don't make the dream so big that it cannot be manifested!*

In Paramhansa Yogananda's autobiography, he tells how Swami Sri Yukteswar would celebrate the solstices and equinoxes. He would lead the chanting devotees through the streets and invite people to the ashram afterwards for a tasty meal. Large crowds would enjoy the food prepared by the ashram residents, and then Sri Yukteswar would speak to them about the universality of the Eternal Religion, *Sanaatan Dharma*.

Inspired by this example, we decided to offer a similar meal and talk at the Seattle community, on the evening of the solstice. When we asked Swami for his thoughts, he encouraged us. Naturally, we couldn't lead a kirtan parade through the streets, but everything else was possible. We prepared a lovely meal and served it free of charge, followed by a fire ceremony and a talk on the universal principles that form the basis of all true religions: Sanaatan Dharma, the Eternal Truth.

It looked, at first, as if only a few people would attend. To our amazement, people then began pouring in—more than ninety people packed into a room that we had set up for forty. The cooks quickly prepared extra food, and a beautiful evening was enjoyed by all.

Later that night, Swami called to ask how it had gone. With wonder in our voices, we told him about the gathering of the large and happy crowd of souls, most of whom were newcomers. Swami replied, "Of course many attended." To him, it was completely natural in light of the heightened energy of the solstice. Our wish to emulate Sri Yukteswar's example, and our willingness to try something entirely new in his name, helped us learn that the natural cycles of the stars can, in fact, influence our lives.

The Seattle community founded a school based on the educational principles of Paramhansa Yogananda, as explained by Swami Kriyananda in his book *Education for Life*.

We started with a preschool, but by the time the first children needed an elementary school, we had no teachers who were trained in the Education for Life principles. After interviewing a number of candidates, we selected a former public school teacher who was willing to give the system a try. When I mentioned to Swami what we were doing, he responded, "Why don't you bring her to see me in California, so I can meet her?"

I knew that she wouldn't be interested, and I also knew that Swami wanted me to understand that the most important qualification for teachers in our system was strong personal spiritual practice, regardless of the teacher's spiritual path. Naturally, he was correct. Several years later, the school had to close for a variety of unrelated reasons, but we had learned a valuable lesson.

It's important to remember that perfection isn't possible on this earthly plane: that, as Swami often reminded us, it is possible only in God. However, what we *can* do in this world is to take one step at a time in the right direction. In testing the possibilities for starting a school, we learned a great deal that would help us when the right time arrived to create something more permanent.

A family in the community complained to Swami that the school tuition was too high for families earning low wages. Swami urged us to consider spreading the school budget among all the residents, not only those with children in the school. I felt that it was an inspired solution, and I championed it. It wasn't popular among some of the residents, however; a compromise of some sort was necessary. Still, I continued to advocate for the initial proposal. Swami then advised me: *Be practical in your idealism.* He would rather abandon an idea than force people to accept it against their will. He was careful to teach us that harmony wins the day.

I've spoken often about how finances were chronically tight in the community. I should clarify that it was not on account of mismanagement, but because we were always trying to accomplish a lot more than we had funds for!

Eventually, the original community grew too large. Swami did two things to resolve the situation. First, he began starting other communities led by people with long experience of life at the original community. Second, he urged us to create smaller neighborhoods within the community. This inspired him to compose the song "Channels," so that each neighborhood could take on one of the nature themes from the song: birds, trees, stars, flowers, mountains, and rivers. This gave it an element of fun. The new "channels,"

as he called them, were smaller mini-communities where meaningful relationships could flourish more easily.

❦

In the early 1980s, Swami founded a community in Italy, near Assisi. We purchased a property with an old hotel on the grounds. My husband oversaw the finances, and he hoped—and prayed—that the work there would take responsibility for the mortgage. Instead, they had to turn to the original community for help. Developing new communities was never simple or easy, but as they expanded, we always tried to stretch as far as possible to help, and we grew spiritually in the process.

The Italian community quickly began to shed a very welcome and beneficial influence on the ones in America. Devotion came much more naturally to the Italians, and a stream of visitors in both directions soon brought about a blend of Italian devotion with American practicality. As the communities helped each other, we learned that the benefits to the original community far outweighed the financial sacrifices.

❦

In the 1980s, new digital technologies for composing music were still in their infancy. Swami was eager to find equipment that could help him compose more efficiently. When someone showed him a new but quite complex system, he was delighted. We often teased him for being a modern Renaissance man, keenly interested in browsing the high-tech stores for gadgetry that could help us offer the teachings.

The equipment cost $28,000, a great deal of money at the time (roughly $82,000 in 2024 dollars). Swami believed that it was the music that most perfectly expressed the vibration of Yogananda, because it spoke to people's hearts more directly than books and lectures could.

We found donations to purchase the equipment, and some of our more tech-savvy members tried their best to understand it, but in the end we were never able to master its use. Afterwards, Swami told us that simply knowing the possibility existed had been worth the price. Years later, he was thrilled to acquire software that was much easier to understand, and that made it effortless to transcribe his inspirations into musical notation.

Sometimes he would find fresh inspiration through contact with some person, or even as in this case through a new technology. People often suggested directions for the work, and he would always consider them with an open mind. He would only follow them, however, if he felt prompted from within to do so.

Negativity blocks the flow of creative inspiration. Work, therefore, with positive people whose desire is to be helpful.

Someone gave Swami $10,000 so that he could take an extended seclusion to write his next book. At the time, I handled his personal finances. On the day the check arrived, a letter came from a nun in the Philippines, telling him how her convent was struggling, and asking if he could help. Without hesitation, Swami turned to me and asked me to send her the $10,000.

Throughout my years with Swami, I saw that even as he worked to develop communities, he was always thinking of how he could give, rather than what he could receive.

My husband and I learned an important lesson early on. It was soon after the fire in 1976. To help fund our efforts to rebuild, and to generate income for residents who had lost their homes, we explored the possibility of opening businesses in nearby Nevada City, California. Swami marched up and down the few streets of the charming town, looking at health food stores, ice cream parlors, cafes, clothing stores, etc.

We decided that we would open a combination health food store and restaurant. We located three storefront spaces next to a successful supermarket. We had planned to lease at most one or two spaces, but when Swami saw them, he suggested that we lease all three. It was a big leap, though, and we ended up starting with just two.

From the day the store opened its doors, it struggled. This

impasse continued for several years under various managers, and then the third space again became available. We were losing money, but remembering Swami's initial suggestion, we took the plunge and leased it. From *that* day onward the store became profitable!

I believe the lesson that Swami wanted us to learn was that a project needs a certain critical mass to generate enough magnetism and momentum to make an impact. Still, he had the courage, and the endless patience, to let us learn from our mistakes.

In the early days of computers, there was a business in the community which was involved with computer hardware and software development. The men who ran it were technically savvy but struggled with the business side. When they asked Swami for his advice, he invited several of us to come to a meeting where the tech folks would talk about their plight.

After their presentation, Swami suggested that instead of developing computer systems, they might go out and teach others what they knew about them. Swami saw with clear intuition that their natures made them unsuited to be businessmen, but that they could be successful as scientists and teachers, and that they weren't likely to succeed if they continued trying to squeeze themselves into the wrong role.

The men were disappointed. They didn't want to move into a new kind of work; they wanted a fix for their struggling enterprise. Sadly, the business failed.

❧

A woman came to the community who had severe mental health issues. She took various prescription medicines to manage her condition. Some of the residents had strong views on healthful eating; they tried to influence her to stop the medications and change her diet. When Swami heard about this, he brought it up at a community gathering. He explained that she needed the medications to be able to function in her day-to-day life, and he encouraged us to understand that a healthy diet wouldn't be sufficient for her. Moreover, the consequences could be grave. His compassionate counsel opened my eyes to the right approach when addressing similar situations in future.

❧

While visiting Swami's home in Gurgaon, India, I was chatting with his cook, Lila, in the kitchen while Swami worked at his desk in another room. At one point, the conversation turned to specialty diets, and I commented that at that moment in the Seattle community, we were grappling with extreme health food fads in the community's kitchen. Just then Swami entered and overheard the last part of our conversation. He said very strongly that we needed to put a stop to it, because, he explained, "People will make food their religion, and not even realize it."

He illustrated the point by telling us how Yogananda was served chicken- instead of cheese enchiladas at a restaurant. Rather than make a fuss, he simply pushed the chicken aside with his fork and ate what he could of the meal.

Unless there are overarching health issues, which can sometimes be the case, Yogananda counseled moderation in diet as in everything else. If we aren't careful, we can find ourselves fretting over an endless list of all the things we're supposed to do and not do: diets, foods, lifestyles, places, people, and things. Moderation and flexibility win the day.

On the day in 1976 that the forest fire destroyed twenty-one of our twenty-two homes, Swami was in Hawaii, working on his autobiography. He immediately returned and gathered the community together for a meeting, where he helped us understand the fire as an opportunity to learn useful spiritual lessons.

On that occasion he said that we were living in "the good old days," and that a time would come when prosperity would be our greatest test.

That glimpse into our future is already in evidence in the wider society. In the same way that children of rich families risk becoming spoiled and feeling entitled, if we aren't challenged in our lives, we risk becoming what Sister Gyanamata, Yogananda's most advanced woman disciple, called "spiritual creampuffs."

There was a woman in the Seattle community who rarely participated in anything, and often criticized whatever we did. On one occasion she complained about the format of our morning meditations. Swami happened to be visiting. When I mentioned her comments, he replied that when people live in a spiritual community and wish to be critical, they invariably try to couch their criticisms in spiritual terms.

As with everything in duality, critique acts as a boomerang, bringing criticism to those who initiate it. Swami's remarks helped me feel compassion for the woman. Her attitude didn't change, unfortunately, and she left the community a short while later.

In the early days of the first community, there was a negative group of residents who didn't want Swami's leadership. They eventually held a meeting where they asked the residents to hear them out. I happened to be with Swami later in the evening, when he remarked that we can never reason with negativity, and that it's a waste of time even to try. He urged us to focus instead on positive energy and solutions, because they will naturally overpower and extinguish the fires of negativity.

Chapter Four
Practical Aspects of Community Life

AFTER THE 1976 fire, about forty of those who'd lost their homes had to move to the nearby town of Nevada City. We were among them, and our new home began to serve as a gathering place for the residents there. Our living room was too small to accommodate everybody, so we looked for an apartment building where we could live together as neighbors. We also needed a more appropriate space for a temple, because our garage, which we had lovingly dubbed "The Garage of the Eternal Religion," had outgrown its usefulness.

In conversation with Swami, we asked for his thoughts on which need we should prioritize. He said that in the ideal order of things, we would look first for a spiritual gathering place, and only then for lodging. It wasn't meant as hard-and-fast advice, but it proved helpful in our case.

We purchased a small church that served us all very well for several years, until those who had been displaced by the fire could build new homes at the original community. The new members who'd been attracted to that church were sufficiently magnetized by the idea of community that they moved to the original community along with the rest of us. The church having at that point served its purpose, we sold it.

Meanwhile, we had found an apartment complex in Grass Valley, adjacent to Nevada City, that seemed ideal, and we invited Swami to see it. As he walked through the apartments, he commented, "Too many walls." He meant that there were too many walls between the residents. Up to that point, all of our city community residences had taken the form of "ashrams," with many residents living in one large home. If the people were separated by so many walls, it might be too easy for them to hide away in their own spaces, an inertia that would prevent them from coming together as a community. Years later, however, when we started urban communities in Palo Alto, Portland, and Seattle, he approved of apartment properties as the only feasible way to have a community in a major metropolitan area.

Support art and artists. Swami placed high value on the arts, and encouraged the communities to do the same. Art brings refinement and sensitivity. It speaks to us through our intuition, enabling the human heart to grasp spiritual concepts with immediacy, without recourse to the rational mind.

American president Theodore Roosevelt said, "A poet can do much more for this country than the proprietor of a nail factory." Our communities have benefited immensely from the performances and works of talented singers, instrumentalists, actors, dancers, writers, and painters. For some, it has been a hobby; for others, their primary source of income. The arts are prized, and weave a richness throughout the community.

In the early 1970s, many of the residents in the original community lived in teepees and trailers, without kitchens. When they wished to use one of the public spaces to offer simple lunches of soup and salad, Swami strongly encouraged them. In this way, we would be certain that everyone could enjoy at least one hearty cooked meal each day.

When I was in my early twenties, I shared an office space with one of the community's leaders. One day, after she and I had been working long hours on a project, we rose from our labors in the mid-afternoon to sit on the outdoor deck of the building and enjoy the view while we ate our lunches.

Just then, Swami came by the office to talk to my friend. When he located us outside, he scolded us gently, saying that the staff looked to my friend for leadership, and that it was important for her to set the pace by arriving on time and having lunch on time. When we tried to explain, our words were lost on him, because of the more important point that he wanted to make. The lesson I took from the experience, which applies equally to meditation, is the importance of doing certain things at the same time each day, to form an unshakable habit. In this case, the issue was to maintain our focus while we worked. As we began to keep regular hours, and as we shared Swami's words with others, the new habit spread throughout the community, bringing a greater sense of purpose, focus, and inner strength.

༶

By the early 1990s, the publishing department that I managed had grown so large that it was housed in five locations around the community. The main office was located near Swami's home, and he liked having it there. The gardens around his home, which was called Crystal Hermitage, were exquisite, and there was a small chapel in a lovely setting, surrounded by flowers and green lawns. One day he held a meeting that included some of us from the publishing department, some of the residents who lived on the Hermitage grounds, and the community's planners. A large map of the grounds lay spread out on a table, and we gathered around.

Swami pointed to a spot next to the chapel and the beautiful grounds, suggesting that it would be nice if the publishing building could be placed there. Gasps were heard all around! Someone said, "But it's so peaceful here. We don't want to dilute it with a busy work environment, do we?"

Practical Aspects of Community Life 53

Swami replied that when he'd lived with Yogananda in his ashram, they all lived, meditated, and worked in the same building, and there was no conflict at all. He explained that we build too many walls and divisions between the various aspects of our lives, when in fact they are one and the same in God. For that reason, it is spiritually helpful to live in a way that encourages openness and flexibility.

༄

By 1999, Swami had founded eight communities on America's West Coast, and a retreat and community near Assisi, Italy. At one point, he asked the community leaders to come to his home near the Assisi community for ten days of discussions, during which we considered many important topics concerning our spiritual lives. An additional topic of importance was his suggestion that we decentralize the financial and legal administration of the communities. Until then, they had been managed from the largest, original community.

He urged us, in addition to devote greater focus to maintaining our spiritual bonds, since this was the most important aspect of our lives together.

Swami understood that in the ascending age in which we live, we will gradually move away from the institutions of the past, and toward a greater emphasis on the spiritual welfare and Self-realization of the individual. Trying to keep a network of communities bound together under a single organizational umbrella would be counter to the natural direction in which the world's consciousness was now moving.

Moreover, it would take us away from the grassroots decision-making that had worked so well for us. We began the process of decentralization right away; it took a few years to complete. The active spiritual cooperation among the communities continued completely naturally.

༄

At the same gathering of leaders in Assisi, Swami said that in the future, when communities would, as Yogananda predicted, "spread like wildfire," each one could specialize in some area that would be useful and inspiring to the whole—for example, healing, music, visual arts, schools, farming, etc.—and that they could exchange goods and services. Swami suggested that we begin to think in this manner now.

༄

Swami rarely used the term or concept "fundraising"; he nearly always talked instead about promotions and giving. He preferred putting out energy and money for others, rather than asking it of them. When funds were urgently needed, he would suggest that I ask a certain person, or several people, for what we required. But he preferred to share the gift of Yogananda's teachings with an attitude of positive expectation, and not of begging: "What comes of itself, let it come."

Swami often quoted Yogananda: "We should organize block by block." It expresses in a nuts-and-bolts way the law of magnetism: that energy given builds even greater energy.

To start a new community, Swami would typically send a small team to the area. In the 1980s, for example, there was already a dynamic meditation group in Seattle. When the members asked Swami to send them a minister to help them become better established, Swami sent *four* ministers. The group was stunned—now they had a staff of four to support! It wasn't at all what they'd expected. However, this was not a church or a parish, but a community. The leaders and ministers therefore needed to have a variety of skills, which usually requires multiple people.

Swami downplayed organizations: Though they are necessary, they are not the definition of a spiritual community. He preferred to think of the communities he founded as a spiritual movement, defined not by its structure but by its spirit.

Although the communities required corporate formats, we were never interested in creating top-down bureaucracies. We preferred a minimum of meetings, usually once a year to adhere to government rules such as the need to nominate a board and officers.

Decisions were generally made at the grassroots level, by those who were directly involved with a particular aspect or project. The typical bureaucratic structure of corporations is incompatible with the best interests of a spiritual community. They work with a hierarchy, and a gradually growing distaste for ceding responsibility to the local level. Decentralization is advisable for any organization, but in spiritual communities it is essential, in order that everyone have the opportunity to work through his karma and learn from his own successes and mistakes.

Swami discouraged us from accepting government funds, as they always come with strings attached. A school or business that accepts government funding will soon find itself having to do whatever the government demands. All the more so in the case of a work such as ours, where, because of constraints on government support to spiritual organizations, we would be forced, step by step and before very long, to forfeit the very heart of our mission.

In the community schools, Swami suggested that we limit dialogue with the parents, and rely instead on educators with long experience of the schools' philosophy and methods. Parents can offer valuable energy, but their theories and preferences regarding the best educational approaches ought not to be imposed on the school.

Swami often reminded us that the school system thriving now for more than fifty years was given to the world by Paramhansa Yogananda, and first expressed in a school that he founded as a young man in India in 1917.

If you ever found yourself at a restaurant table with Swami, the bill would always be split equally regardless of the size of the group, to make it easier on the waitstaff, and to foster a spirit of cooperation. This could sometimes come as a surprise to those not accustomed to Swami's approach to restaurant meals!

When Swami was a young monk, Yogananda told him that he hoped the men and women monastics would one day have their own separate living quarters. Some years after Yogananda's passing, Swami asked for funds to build a men's dormitory. When the request was declined, he was inspired to import harmoniums from India and sell them. Even though the income was small at best, it was energy output that he felt would magnetize a divine response; it was, moreover, all he could do, as a monk receiving an allowance of $10 a month. Soon after he began his little business, someone made a large donation, part of which went to build that dormitory.

We've seen the same principle in action again and again in the communities. In response to energy put out, more energy is created.

Chapter Five

Attitudes for Living in Community

PARAMHANSA YOGANANDA HAD a saying of spiritual encouragement: *"A saint is a sinner who never gave up."* While it's relatively easy to apply this adage to ourselves, it's essential in a spiritual community to hold this attitude also toward others. We have come together to support one another in the journey to spiritual perfection. What counts is one's sincerity of effort. Viewing others in this way, we don't hold false expectations of them. Instead, we mirror to them the encouragement that Yogananda offered to us all.

Perseverance is an essential quality for living in a spiritual community. It is healthy to see our efforts as directional. So long as we make even incremental progress in the right direction, success will be ours. Even if we fail along the way, we can take great comfort in knowing that there will be far more days when we'll be successful, so long as we persevere and keep trying.

Many years ago, I was living in a community that found itself teetering on the brink of disaster because of its financial structure. The community property was a 5.5-acre apartment complex, owned by a group of investors, some of whom had sold their homes to invest in the community.

A number of the investors were on different spiritual paths from that of the original community, and wanted a say in organizing the community to their liking. Having lived for several decades at the original community, I had learned that although all true paths are good, each community must focus on one path to avoid conflict and confusion. Things finally came to a head: About half of the residents decided to sell their investments and move on. It caused a major crisis, since we didn't have the money to buy their shares, and it seemed the community might need to be dissolved.

When several of us met to discuss the situation, we commented that even if the community were destroyed, we would simply pick up what was left, stay together, and form a new community elsewhere. In other words, community is spirit, not the physical location.

In the end, the crisis was revealed as an opportunity for a miracle. On the very day that we began receiving formal notices of the dissidents' intention to leave, a number of wonderful prospective residents called us, one by one, and asked if they could invest and move in. In the end, those who moved away received their investments back, and those who moved in were thrilled to be part of a spiritual community and live among friends who shared their path. By keeping our faith strong, we learned, yet again, that good efforts and intentions were joined to higher forces, and that "someone else" was ultimately in charge.

❦

Always be willing to examine your first principles. Swami Kriyananda often spoke of this as a way of staying flexible, and being willing to turn on a dime should it become apparent that we've begun moving in the wrong direction.

❦

Swami used to say, "*Every word matters.*" He counseled us to say only that which would be helpful. Living in the close quarters of a spiritual community, it's even more important in what we say to be careful, sensitive to the feelings of others, and respectful of their current level of understanding. This reflects Swami's definition of maturity: *the ability to relate to realities other than our own.*

If we wish to get along with others and create harmonious friendships, it is critical to choose our words with care. This is true in all meaningful relationships. People often fall into the habit of saying whatever comes to mind, but it is a sign of maturity to speak only when appropriate, and always in a way that will be helpful to whomever we're speaking to.

❦

Swami would occasionally invite my husband and me to be present when he counseled someone. Two occasions stand out.

The first involved a man who wanted to leave his marriage for another woman. He and his new girlfriend had come to Swami for his guidance. Two other couples, longtime leaders in the community, were also present. Once we were gathered in the living room, Swami entered, and without sitting down, walked over, greeted us all, and said, "If you would like to pursue this relationship, you will need to do it in another one of our communities." He then turned and went back to his apartment downstairs. The couple did move to another community, and before long the relationship fell apart.

The second occasion involved a man serving in an important role in the community. He had been feeling unhappy with the challenges of his job, and had asked if he could take another position. Again, Swami came in after our small party had gathered. This time he sat down, looked at the man, and said, "Yogananda would not be pleased if you left this post." He then stood and returned to his apartment.

For several decades thereafter, the man remained in that position, where he provided the firm foundation the department needed to thrive. Nevertheless, in my years with Swami, I observed that he *never* prioritized the success of a project, department, or other endeavor over the spiritual needs of the individual. In this case, fortunately, both were served.

I often wondered why Swami invited us to those meetings. I've since come to understand that, in both cases, while he could have said a great deal more, further words would not have helped.

Swami said only what was needed, leaving it to those involved to make their decision.

Swami didn't always counsel people so abruptly. He was compassionate when compassion was called for, and he was a powerful listener.

When emotions were running high, however, he knew that the most effective medicine was to be found in silent inner communion with God.

He always held out to us the truth that understanding only ever truly comes in that way. In the two cases I've described, "the writing was on the wall," and he knew that the solution could only come from within.

Forty years after those, as well as many other meetings, I've begun teaching a course on spiritual counseling, and I'm profoundly grateful for the many glimpses Swami gave me into intuitive counseling.

◈

I shared a small section of the office building with a woman who had given several years of service as a community leader. The office had a large window through which we could see the entrance to the community in the distance. One day, when Swami came by, he walked into our little office and, leaning over behind the woman, looked out the window. Then, mimicking her attitude, he said, "Who is *that*? What are *they* doing here?" She immediately understood: *Never judge*. Always keep an open attitude to those who enter. As an Indian saying puts it, "The guest is God."

❧

To the membership committee in the original community Swami said, "Don't allow people to talk about problems too much, lest it affirm the problems into reality!" He explained that this is the nature of emotions: We are not helping people when we allow them too much emotional expression. He advised us, in counseling people, to pray inwardly for solutions, then try to insert the solutions at the right moment, to redirect the conversation.

❧

Never force or impose your will on others. Instead, work with those who *want* to accept your ideas.

❧

In a community, not everyone has to "be on board." Consensus is *not* the model for spiritual communities: grassroots decision-making is.

❧

Never base decisions concerning membership in a community—or any other decision, for that matter—on a person's finances.

❧

Attitudes for Living in Community 65

A man who worked in a department I managed had been with us for no more than a few months when he was laid up with severe back pain. The department ran on a tight budget, but Swami urged me to keep paying him. Each month, I would check with Swami, and each time he would say the same thing, even though I had to hire another person to fulfill the man's tasks. This went on for more than six months. Finally, the situation was resolved when the man moved away to live with his family. I realized that Swami was teaching me an important lesson: to look beyond the practical, toward compassion—to live, in other words, by our ideals.

I observed that Swami would often wait years before he suggested an idea, whether to an individual or to the whole community. At other times, he wouldn't suggest an idea publicly at all, if he felt that people weren't ready to hear it. *Patience is the shortest path to God.*

Someone of our publishing staff was on a sales trip to Los Angeles, when a major earthquake struck the suburb of Northridge. The man called and said that he wasn't injured, and that he planned to come home. When I told Swami, he had me get the man on the phone, and told him to remain and complete the sales trip as planned.

The man was stunned. "But Swami," he said, "the stores are all in disarray! The staffs are busy putting their products back on the shelves!" Swami replied that it was important not to give in to the destructive force of the earthquake, but to rise above it. He should complete the trip in order to keep his commitment to his word. And he should go to the stores and help the employees put them in order.

It was a profound lesson: that we need to put our beliefs into action, even in challenging circumstances, through *courage in selfless service*.

A man in the community had built his own home as best he could. The construction wasn't ideal—he wasn't a carpenter—and when he decided to move, he put a high price on the house. There was a family that needed a home and wanted to purchase it, but they had four children and not much money. The housing committee felt that the price would set a bad precedent, and they asked the man to lower it.

Swami called the committee members together and urged them to allow this man to ask the price he wanted. He had put his heart into it, and fully believed he was putting a fair value on his labor; he couldn't understand the committee's claims to the contrary. If forced to lower the price, he would feel that he'd been unfairly treated, and leave on a sour note. *The heart of the law is mercy.* Was not that the more important precedent to set?

Attitudes for Living in Community 67

Again and again, I saw that Swami would never negotiate or try to get a seller to lower a fixed price. Whatever they asked, he paid. After all, it was only money.

When asked to work on a project, support an idea, or participate in anything at all, say "YES!" first, and put your whole heart into it. There will be plenty of time later to analyze the cons. If we begin by listing the reasons it might not work, the balloon will never get off the ground. Saying "Yes!" affirms the openness that is essential for allowing creative solutions to flow through us. Swami's philosophy was simple: "Say *Yes* to life!"

When Swami gave a public program, and people asked how many had attended, he would give the highest possible estimate. And with each new book, he would tell us, "We will sell a million!" It was only after years that I realized the connection to how Swami actually saw *us*: He saw the highest in us and ignored everything else. He related to us not as "saints in the making," but as saints *already*.

Some people believe they are being realistic in seeing both the problems and solutions in each situation. Swami was aware of the problems, but rarely voiced them. His focus was instead entirely on solutions. I recall one occasion when someone in our department was holding himself up as an expert and wanted a role in a project. When he asked Swami to give him the role, I felt that I should alert Swami to my misgivings. But before I could say a word, he said, "I know." I continued to speak, and after a few more words, he again said, "I know." He was trying to spare me the reciting of the problems, but he was also telling me that he was fully aware of the issues, but that he had deliberately chosen to direct his energy and attention to helping this person instead. The lesson was clear. As Swami often reminded us, the rational mind is problem-oriented, but divine intuition—the superconscious mind—is solution-oriented. Thus, his advice when approaching any project or problem: "*Be solution-oriented.*"

When Swami spoke of the importance of harmony and cooperation in our relationships, especially in a spiritual community, he would sometimes tell the story of an old man in India who lay on his deathbed. He had six sons, and he asked each of them to go outside and get a stick. When they returned, he asked them to try to break the stick, and they were easily able to do so. He then asked them to go and find another stick, and he asked the strongest of them to hold all of the sticks together in a bundle and try to break them. When he was unable to do so, the father explained that if they went off on their own, they might easily be broken, but if they stayed together in harmony and cooperation, nothing and no one would be able to break them.

Attitudes for Living in Community

In the mid-1970s I was one of the few people in the original community who owned a car. One day, I was asked to pick up a visitor from the bus station in Grass Valley, seventeen miles away. I was in my twenties and had studied at the University of California in Berkeley, where I had seen many hippies. The young man I picked up had long hair, slovenly clothing, and smelled as though he hadn't bathed in weeks. For those reasons I formed an immediate dislike for him.

Later, after Swami gave the talk at Sunday service, I saw him speaking with the man. Swami was looking deeply into his eyes and seemed thoroughly engrossed in their conversation. In Swami's eyes I saw not a hint of judgment. He was listening as intently as to a most trusted friend. I immediately saw my error in judging the man for superficial reasons that had nothing to do with his true, soul nature as a child of God.

Paramhansa Yogananda trained Swami not to allow inertia to take hold in his activities. In Swami's autobiography, *The New Path,* he included a note from Yogananda in which he asked: "How much have you edited? *Thorough* but *fast* editing is necessary, or nothing will be done. Time is scant." In another note, he said, "Do not procrastinate or act carelessly. Hurry with discretion." Swami learned to do things immediately, before inertia could interfere.

Swami would often give me instructions for a project or send me a partial manuscript to read. He would then call after thirty minutes to see if I had finished it! It was his way of teaching me not to let inertia set in, and to complete my tasks immediately: to "Do it NOW!" It was an admonition to which he devoted an entire book by that title.

❧

Swami taught us: Don't do something only because you will set an example—do it because it's the right thing to do.

❧

When Swami was ill, people would send him recommendations for an endless variety of alternative remedies. At these times his dining table would be heaped with a mountainous pile of those remedies. Some likely conflicted with his medications, yet he would try many of them, not out of concern for his health, but in a spirit of *open-mindedness*. He was willing to try all manner of healing modalities, while retaining a deep respect for traditional, Western allopathic medicine.

❧

Some communities, to ensure that the members are all moving forward in accordance with their shared ideals, create elaborate rules and systems, or demand that each decision be approved by unanimous consensus. But the spiritual path is individual: what's right depends, for each of us, on where we are along the pathway to our ultimate Self-realization.

Therefore, Swami recognized the importance of *self-motivation*. No one would force you to get out of bed and meditate, or take a specific job, or require you to participate in a community workday. Swami showed us that our individual choices and decisions must always be based on convictions that come from within us.

When a couple in the original community divorced, one of them left the community. At a small gathering soon after, Swami said to the spouse, out of the blue: "He should always feel welcome to come back." Indeed, when any resident moved away, the door always remained open for him. And if he did ever return, Swami was ever gracious, warm and kind as if he had never left.

Someone attacked Swami's character. In my effort to defend him, in my response I included the phrase, "He (Swami) never said that he was perfect." The next day, Swami sent me a short paper saying that he found the expression unfortunate. It could be taken to suggest (unintentionally, of course) that his faults were "so glaring as to be better left undescribed"!

He went on to explain, "To emphasize a person's lack of perfection is not the way to affirm God's love for all of us. What it does is emphasize our distance from Him. Our real need is quite the opposite. As St. Teresa of Avila put it to the nuns in her charge, 'I don't want to hear any of you saying, "I'm no saint." We are here to *become* saints!' "

Swami concluded, "Best it would be, I should think, to say, 'I don't expect perfection in others, though I hope to achieve it for myself someday, in God. Meanwhile, I am grateful when someone inspires me to become a better person, and a truer devotee.' "

❧

In the early days of our residential community in Seattle, Swami would call several times a week to support us and answer our questions. At one point, we faced extremely difficult financial hurdles. I didn't want to burden Swami, knowing that thousands were always heaping their troubles on him. But when a friend told him our community was on the brink of economic disaster, he replied that it could not be the case, or we would have told him about it. So when I saw him, I laid everything on the table. He said, essentially, Just keep doing what you are doing and all will be well.

I understood this to be the way that we should behave with God. We should not cherry-pick some limited subset of matters to share with Him in prayer, but rather lay every aspect of our lives at the feet of the Divine. In God, all things are neutral. It is only our judgment that makes them seem good or bad.

Swami often said, "*If the spirit is right, everything will turn out as it should.*" Look within, he was saying, and if you feel God's presence, don't be concerned about what appears to be happening on the outside. His unworried response to our community's seemingly dire finances reminded me that when we worry, we can never be in tune with divine energy, which is always solution-oriented. Worry is a negative emotion laden with negative energies. They disturb our thoughts, feelings, and actions, making us restless and disturbed. "*Be in tune*," Paramhansa Yogananda used to say, that is what is most important.

༄

Sometimes, if we became preoccupied with mundane details, Swami would say: "You don't want your tombstone to read, 'He paid his bills'—do you?"

༄

After the forest fire in 1976, Swami led a community meeting to discuss how we could earn the money to rebuild. When he invited our ideas, I raised my hand and suggested that a few small groups could go out to the city, rent houses, get jobs, live simply, and send home their excess money.

Swami didn't accept or reject my suggestion, but he invited other ideas. In the end, the proposal that won the day was for a large group of strong, sturdy souls to apply for tree-planting contracts with the Forest Service. Several others would go along to cook and maintain the campsite. It was suggested that we could earn lots of money in this way. I had my doubts, and I didn't have much hope for the plan, but Swami was enthusiastic. He even drove to the tree-planters' camp several times to offer them inspiration. Then he would come home and rave about the beautiful spirit he had seen.

When all was said and done, not only did the tree planters not come home with extra funds to rebuild, they acquired debt in the process. Still, Swami spoke glowingly of the good spirit the project had generated.

I learned important lessons in the months and years after the fire. Going to the city and pooling our funds would have been inadvisable. The pull of the world might have drawn the less committed away. And the expectation of pooling income would have been contrary to the spirit of freedom for everyone to decide individually what he would give or not give.

If the spirit is right, everything will turn out as it should. It isn't necessary that things work out the way we think they should. It's necessary only that they work out as Divine Mother wishes. The spirit of cooperation at the tree-planting camp was beautiful. In the end, all of the donations, people, and resources came to us that we needed to rebuild. When we put out energy with faith, in a spirit of enthusiastic, loving service, our efforts are bound to bear fruit, although not always in the manner we expected.

In the early 1970s, Swami often mentioned Paramhansa Yogananda's predictions of troubled times ahead for the world. He spoke of investing money in gold or silver so that the money would keep its value.

At the time, my total funds were $1,500, which would be worth almost $12,000 in 2024.

I decided to purchase gold with all of it, and buried it next to my rustic cottage. Years later, in June 1976, a larger cottage came up for sale at the property five miles down the road (where the main community was now located), and I decided to dig up the gold and buy it. It was exactly the right amount! The family that lived in the cottage planned to move to the city in about a week. Three days after I paid them in full, the forest fire swept through the community, burning up twenty-one of our twenty-two homes, including the one I had just paid for! None of us were insured, so I lost everything.

My takeaway was that *my security rests in God alone*. There was another important lesson about a year later. Soon after the fire, I moved temporarily to the beautiful area of Carmel, California, to take a job and replenish my funds. I met my future husband, who ended up hiring me, and we eventually moved back to the community together (when some of the donations, along with funds of our own, made it possible to rebuild part of my house), where we raised two beautiful children.

There were hidden blessings yet unseen, just behind the seeming destruction of the fire. Throughout this time I remember feeling only a sense of deep inner peace. Swami helped us to see the tests of this difficult time as blessings from the Divine, and for me the blessings were palpable.

꽃

One day I was feeling particularly tense at work. A gathering was scheduled at Swami's home at the end of the workday, and of course I went. At one point, Swami and I passed through the same double doorway. With a twinkle in his eyes, he put his hands on his shoulders, raised them and squished his shoulders with tension, then relaxed them, and walked on, without a word. He had mirrored my tension so that, becoming aware of it, I could release it. *The best lessons may be transmitted in silence.*

꽃

The governing council of the community normally met at the main offices, but on one occasion we held a meeting at Swami's home. The man who ran the dairy arrived late in his work clothes, which were very dirty. Swami stopped the meeting and asked him to go home and change, as he wasn't dressed appropriately to come to his home for the meeting. The man did as Swami asked. I realized that our clothing conveys a vibration, and that the vibrations of a dairy might not be appropriate in an office. Moreover, the clothes we wear convey respect, perhaps not to the cows, but certainly to the humans we interact with.

Attitudes for Living in Community

༄༅

When our two children were in their infancy, I struggled to maintain a regular Kriya Yoga meditation practice. I was often exhausted from lack of sleep and constant nursing. One day, my path happened to cross with Swami's. He asked me how I was doing, and when I told him about my exhaustion and my struggles to practice Kriya, to my amazement he replied, "Do Kriya *while you're nursing!*"

This teaching applies in many other situations. Never think we can't do our spiritual practices: Whatever our tests, make modifications as needed to keep our daily meditative appointment with God, regardless of the circumstances or how exhausted we feel. This principle applies not only to our spiritual practices but to every aspect of our lives. As my husband likes to say, "Both-And!"

༄༅

Once a new woman moved to the community who was originally from Europe. I met her and found her to be lovely. Later in the day, I mentioned the encounter to Swami, and he asked me the woman's name. I told him that it was Karen, but that she spelled it Karin. He asked how she pronounced it, and when I told him I wasn't sure, his response was interesting. He said, "Well let's find out and make sure. It is important that we pronounce it the way she wishes us to."

Reading between the lines, I understood: *Be respectful of each individual.* It was a quality that he modeled constantly before us, and it's an attitude essential, also, to preserving harmony in a community.

PART 2

Living the Inner Life

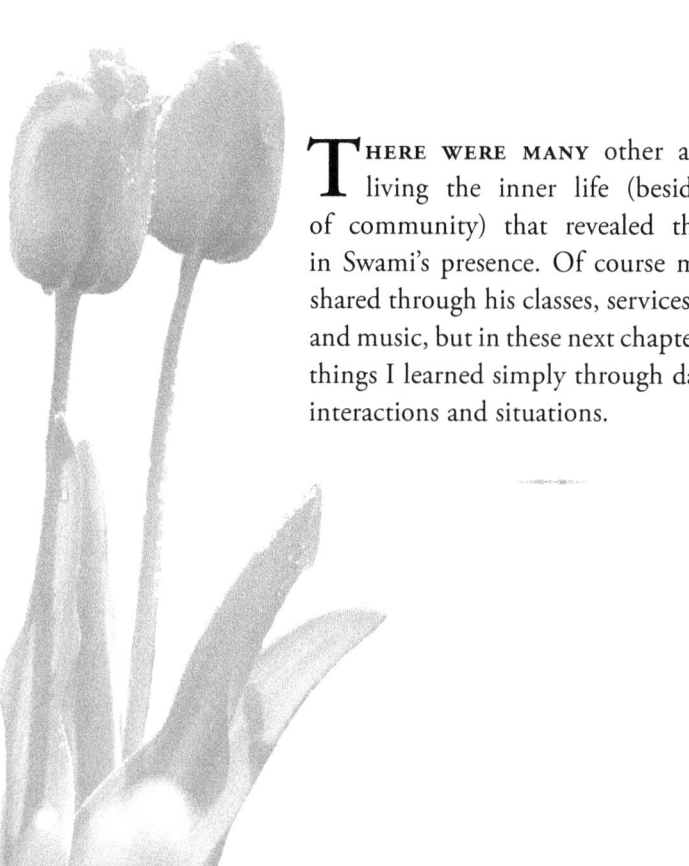

There were many other aspects of living the inner life (besides those of community) that revealed themselves in Swami's presence. Of course much was shared through his classes, services, lectures, and music, but in these next chapters I share things I learned simply through day-to-day interactions and situations.

Chapter Six
Meditation, Concentration, and Devotion

ONE TIME I was at Swami's and followed him to his downstairs apartment for a meeting. We passed through the living room of his dome, which was evidently set up for group chanting (*kirtan*). Swami commented casually, "Kirtans should be half chanting and at least half meditation. After all, the purpose of chanting is to lead us into meditation."

After the fire at the original community, there were more than forty of us living "in town" while our houses were slowly rebuilt. My husband and I met Swami in front of an older church we were thinking of buying as a place to gather for meditation and yoga.

We arrived early, and the realtor was late. I clutched a clipboard (as one might clutch schoolbooks) with the "for sale" flyer and the realtor's business card. That position soon became tiring, so I simply held it under my arm. After a wait of about twenty minutes, I suggested that we find a pay phone and call the realtor (this was long before cell phones).

Swami had barely glanced at the clipboard while I held it upside down, and then only for a few seconds, but to my amazement he recited the realtor's phone number! When we exclaimed at this feat of memory, he explained that it was simply a matter of learning to *focus*.

A side note is that we lost the negotiation for the church. Later, Swami remarked that the offer my husband and I had made was too low, which was why we lost the negotiation. The lesson has remained with me. Through the years, we've had numerous opportunities to purchase properties, and thankfully those purchases succeeded.

Swami told us that Yogananda discouraged his disciples from having surgery anywhere along the center of the body. The spine is a sensitive area spiritually, he explained, so unless the condition is life threatening, surgery is best avoided.

At one point, Swami had a deviated septum (the membrane separating the nostrils), which required surgery. Remembering his guru's caution, he decided to have it done without anesthesia. Later he told us that the surgeon was perspiring with nervousness, although he himself remained calm and contented. He recognized the experience as painful, but chose not to define it as pain.

Swami routinely refused novocaine for dental procedures; he diverted his mind from the pain by focusing instead on mentally composing music, for example. *Mind over matter* was a skill that Swami had mastered. He could not have transcended the pain had his mind not been completely focused, and his heart open to divine grace.

In Yogananda's spiritual tradition, the practice of Hatha Yoga (postures) includes devotion. The purpose of Hatha Yoga is to prepare the body to remain still during meditation. Meditation too, practiced properly, includes devotion. When the heart is thus purified, upliftment comes naturally.

Swami learned from Yogananda to do every task quickly and efficiently, *with concentration*. In managing his projects, he assigned himself a seemingly endless stream of self-imposed deadlines. By setting this example, he showed us how we, too, by focusing our energy, could complete any task we set ourselves.

Meditation and God-remembrance, also, require focused attention. Thus our daily activities give us many opportunities to deepen our meditation by learning to concentrate.

We learned from Swami also that concentration comes easily and naturally when our heart's feelings are engaged. It's much easier to keep our attention on what we're doing when we are enthusiastic, and driven by a strong *desire* to accomplish the task at hand.

Chapter Seven
Satsang (Fellowship)

WHEN I'D GO to Swami's home to discuss a problem in our department, he was usually busy writing or composing music. With a kindly wave of his hand, he would silently invite me to take a seat. I would sit for a few minutes in the tangible peace and calmness.

Finally, he would turn and ask me what I wished to tell him. And each time, though I searched my mind, I would be unable to remember what it was I had come to discuss. In his uplifted presence, it was simply impossible to think of problems! Yogananda used to say that the company we keep is of utmost importance to our success in the spiritual life—and this is a good example of it.

Universality: After Swami moved to India in 2003 to help make Paramhansa Yogananda better known, we visited him perhaps seven times. During one trip, he required some medical tests the day we arrived, and he invited us to come along. Thus we found ourselves in a small, crowded waiting room in a spotlessly clean, beautiful hospital in Delhi.

Swami immediately began conversing with a family seated next to us; they were Muslims from Bangladesh, and Swami told them that his guru was from Bengal. Swami then burst into song, a Bengali song that Yogananda had sung while Swami was living with him. Although it had been fifty years, he was able to sing it as Yogananda had, recalling every word and note.

The man was moved to tears. Keep in mind that the family were Muslims, and this was a Hindu devotional song to the Divine Mother. Swami sweetly spoke to them about Yogananda, and then reached into his pocket for a small book of slokas from the Bhagavad Gita (a famous Indian scripture) that he had just written. He gave them the book, and the man held it to his heart and expressed deep gratitude.

Swami was not proselytizing: simply offering kindness and friendship. These two men on different paths were beautiful expressions of the universal Spirit. In its highest octave, *fellowship* is universal, since we recognize the innate essence at the heart of each person as one and the same.

꧁꧂

Toward the end of his life, Swami made a strong and compelling appeal to us to offer more in-person courses around the U.S., and not limit our outreach to online courses alone. In a letter to the leaders, eight years before the Covid pandemic, he said, "Online is not the way to go, and even as an adjunct I consider it a feeble one."

I interpreted this to mean that online is a difficult way to exchange spiritual vibrations from soul to soul.

Swami used video and audio extensively to record and share the teachings. When he began teaching in India, he recorded over a thousand classes and programs for television, but he didn't warm up to online programming in the same way as personal appearances. He missed the vibrational exchange of those wonderful meetings, which were attended by thousands. Many of those who've attended the online presentations by my husband and me have also expressed a longing for a personal contact.

In his letter, Swami continued: "Personal contact has the required immediacy. It works. I've proved that it works." He went on to encourage us to appeal to new teachers with these words: "Please, everyone: The world needs our help! You don't need a long course of study to start out. Start with what you have. Watch and learn from the videos of my classes. But you know enough already, surely, to help people who don't know these teachings at all!"

At school meetings in the original community, parents with different approaches to raising children would become vocal. Their conflicting strong opinions threatened our progress toward creating a clear expression of Yogananda's educational ideals.

Swami remarked that the mere fact that parents have a child doesn't automatically make them experts at raising or educating children. Personal attachments and prejudices, negative emotions, and other currents are often at play. He encouraged us to find people who were good with children, and to have the children spend more time in activities with them during school hours and afterward. He knew that their goodness and kindness would aid powerfully in magnetizing the children to the right spirit. It was yet another example of the importance of keeping good company.

꧂

Albert Einstein showed us that we are not our bodies; we are energy. Vibration is energy, and the vibrations of our surroundings influence our consciousness. Swami told us that when we are in a mode of receiving or taking-in, such as when we are eating, we absorb the vibrations not only of the food, but also of our surroundings. Therefore, he said, it is important to be selective about the restaurants we choose, and to bring along high-minded friends to surround ourselves with.

꧂

When my husband and I were married, Swami officiated. In his talk, he cited the familiar counsel: "Never say never. Never say always." If we ask someone to do something and he opts not to, for example, it is very tempting to say, "You *never* do it!" Similarly, if someone does something we don't care for, we might say, "You *always* do that!"—even though he may have done it only once or twice. It's important, Swami emphasized, not to put people (or ourselves) into boxes—including our spouse! He added that while this is particularly true for marriage, it is equally applicable for success in any relationship, whether at work, or with friends, community, or family.

As situations arose through the years where we might have been tempted to use those phrases, we would catch ourselves and have a good laugh about it. The marriage guidance worked: it helped us to keep our sense of humor!

Swami was concerned that the various communities might begin to pull away from one another. He therefore urged the leaders to come together once or twice each year for key events in which we would all participate. Harmony is the watchword.

One year we reached a critical turning point regarding the bank construction loan for the temple in Washington, just as our communities' biggest, annual gathering was about to begin in California. Swami had begun to call us daily, some days twice, to make sure we were coming and to ask when we would arrive. But our hands were tied: The bank kept asking for more and more information, and the contractor was anxiously waiting to get started. In the end, we missed the event, and although we later traveled to California to visit Swami, we missed the opportunity to see the other community leaders, who were old friends. There is a palpable exchange of energy that happens when we gather in person, which is important to nurture, and we had missed that. We understood that it was spiritually very important. We haven't missed such an occasion since.

Chapter Eight

Selfless Service

When Swami put me in charge of his special projects, we often worked late into the night. Now and then, he would say, "Thank you for helping." Sometimes he was overseas and not present to be working on the project, but he would call to say, "Thank you for helping."

In time, I came to understand his meaning. An ideal attitude we can have is one of helping God. In everything we do, we are serving as His instruments. Thus, in thanking me, Swami was drawing my awareness to the reality that I was an instrument for God, and for that I am eternally grateful.

When my husband first moved to the original community, he and I managed all of the communities' finances. In a community of spiritual people, financial jobs were not exactly coveted. Finally, we decided to speak with Swami and tell him how difficult it was for us to do these jobs, day in and out. Swami's response was: "You'd better learn to like it!"

His response immediately jolted us out of self-pity and self-involvement, and helped us turn our attention to offering selfless service in a manner that we were blessed to be qualified to do.

༄

The forest fire in 1976 brought many lessons. I've mentioned some already. An additional lesson was in regard to something we called the Joy Tour.

When the fire struck, Swami was away from the community in seclusion, writing his autobiography, *The Path*.* He returned to the community to offer what assistance he could, then went back to complete the book. He knew that thousands would be served through the blessings of that book, and he was determined to finish it on the schedule he had set himself.

Once the book went to the printer, Swami proposed going on a tour around the country (the Joy Tour) as a way to help us rebuild after the fire. Those of us who worked with the community's finances saw this as a dicey proposition at best. We knew from experience that touring was expensive; earning funds beyond covering the tour expenses was not likely. We tried to convey this to Swami, but he wasn't convinced. Someone donated a motorhome, and he embarked on the tour with a group of singers, musicians, and helpers. Their selfless sharing provided spiritual inspiration to the many hundreds who attended the programs.

---

* Later he edited the book extensively and retitled it *The New Path*.

Predictably, the tour cost much more than the income it brought in. What was *not* predicted was that quite a few of the attendees decided to move to the California community, and that some of them would, in time, emerge as community leaders who still live there today. Service, first, last, and always. The benefits of this tour far outweighed the financial considerations. The Joy Tours live on as a cherished landmark memory in the hearts of those who took part in them, and of all those others whose lives were changed as a result. They live on also as a testament to the importance of seeking serviceful, creative solutions to seeming problems. When in doubt: Give.

Swami always answered his phone himself. No matter what he was doing, or with whom he was meeting, when his phone rang, he would answer it. He was always present for those who needed his help. I came to understand that this was true service, and that it was how God works—God is *always* there for us.

When I managed the publishing department, Swami encouraged our staff to consider creating a separate department for each book. Such new departments would provide new avenues for selfless service, and generate income for the residents and the community. And having each department concentrate on a single book would give it focus. In particular, since no two of Swami's books targeted quite the same group of people, it would allow the staff to dive deeply into a variety of ways to reach that book's unique audience.

Consider as an example Swami's book, *The Art of Supportive Leadership*. The staff would focus not only on getting it into bookstores and libraries. They could communicate also with large companies, university business schools, and national business support and teaching organizations about our giving programs based on the book's unique message, thus teaching them how to spread the relevant practices among their ranks.

༄

The community's retreat struggled, in the face of financial obstacles, to keep its doors open. It was determined that carrying salaries and utilities all winter long was the culprit. Since very few people came to the retreat during winter, it was suggested that we close the retreat during the "off season."

When Swami heard about this proposal, he encouraged us to keep it open year round, whatever sacrifices it might entail. "Having the doors open," he said, "expresses the spirit that the guest is God." Although closing for the winter might be the financially sound decision, he was reminding us of a teaching of the Indian scriptures, that when a lesser duty (paying the bills) conflicts with a higher duty (The Guest is God), the lower ceases to be a duty.

❧

Never impose your help on others. Ask first, "How may I help you?" Then wait to hear their response. This was Swami's priceless guidance for leaders everywhere. In a spiritual community especially, it can be easy to make the mistake of assuming that others will welcome our assistance. It's always appropriate to ask, and then to listen sensitively to their response before we say or do anything.

❧

In the early 1980s, Swami invited about a dozen community members to vacation with him in Hawaii. My husband and I were included; our children, ages two and four, would stay with my parents. The vacation sounded glorious! I was so excited by the prospect of reading for long periods without interruption from our little ones that I put together a stack of about five thick spiritual books. When Swami saw my stack, he said, "You can't read spiritual books in Hawaii. All you can do in that tropical paradise is rest. Instead, bring light, easy reading."

The entire vacation was a lesson in service that I like to call "tense and relax." When we serve, it's important to focus. Focus need not involve tension. Still, periodically it is equally important to relax deeply, without focus. Our nature is such that we need to remind ourselves deliberately that it's equally proper to feel fine about focus and relaxation, lest our focus become tension.

During that same vacation in Hawaii, our group occupied condos, with four of us in each unit, while Swami stayed in a house a few miles away, as he hoped to have a break from the constant flow of people needing his help. On the second day, some of us went to the supermarket, where a woman asked if we were from the same community as Swami. She recognized us from a photo she'd seen.

She explained that Swami had called her the day before (he'd gotten her name and contact information from the community's mailing list) and arranged to offer a gathering at her home that evening for all of her friends on the island. She kindly invited us to come. We shouldn't have been surprised that Swami had done this, as it was his nature to serve, although we had sincerely hoped he would rest. Nevertheless, we realized that for Swami, selfless service *was* restful.

During a visit to the Seattle community, Swami stayed at an airport hotel, because he had an early flight the next morning. We decided to keep him company, so we took a room across the hall. The porter who helped us was a Muslim, originally from Kashmir. Swami fell into a long conversation with him, as he'd spent time in Kashmir and had beautiful memories of it.

It turned out that the man was struggling to make a living in the United States. Swami introduced him to us and told him that we lived locally. He encouraged us to exchange contact information and to help the man's family in any way we could. We were able to introduce him to the manager of our book and gift store, who helped him arrange a special showing of Kashmiri imports for the store's customers. The event was a success, and we repeated it several times. The point of this story is to keep an open heart for the stranger, and offer friendship and service whenever possible.

On another occasion, I was traveling with Swami to New York, where he would speak at a New Thought expo. After the porter showed us to our rooms, Swami looked for his wallet to give him a tip. When Swami was out of earshot, the porter turned to me and whispered, "He must be an important person. Who is he?" He had sensed Swami's dignity during the short walk to the room.

Swami had accepted the invitation to the expo as a service. When we see all that we do as a selfless service to the Divine in others, then graciousness surrounds all we do and becomes tangible.

Chapter Nine
Non-Attachment, Renunciation, Expansion

From the beginning of the Ananda communities, inner renunciation played a very important role. Non-attachment is a key precept for those practicing raja yoga. Swami encouraged not only monastics, but also families to practice inner renunciation regardless of what outer lifestyle suited us. Some saints in India were born in wealthy families, yet they had great spiritual depth. Christ did not look to the career or surroundings (positive or negative) of those he taught, but only to their sincerity and spiritual hunger. I observed Swami be the same whether in opulent or humble surroundings, always calmly centered within. Yogananda stayed in the best hotels during his tours. Even when his ashram was nearby in Los Angeles, he would sometimes stay at the Biltmore Hotel. He had his reasons, and he could walk away from it all in the blink of an eye, the test of true renunciation.

When Swami first built the area at Ananda Village called Crystal Hermitage, its sheer size and cost was controversial amongst some. He had used his inheritance, and it became the spiritual center of the community. Little did we know that he was looking into the future, when tens of thousands would flock to the Crystal Hermitage to feel the peace and witness its beauty and dignity. It was not built from desire, but in service to others.

We visited Swami in India in 2007, and during our visit he was diagnosed with colon cancer. It required surgery, and he invited us to accompany him to the hospital. At the appointed time, when the staff came to take him into surgery, several of us were sitting in his room with him. Some of us were meditating, and a couple of us (including Swami) were reading. When I asked him what he was reading on his iPad, he said, "*Samadhi*," a poem by Yogananda that describes the experience of samadhi, divine inner oneness with God.

I found it instructive in two ways. First, Swami was focused on placing his consciousness in the highest state of inner expansion, in preparation for a challenging surgery. Second, I believe Swami was gently reminding us that when we face a great test, we can draw upon this exquisite poem for reassurance and upliftment. Yogananda had suggested to the monks in his ashram that they memorize the poem and recite it daily. I knew that Swami, though he'd been reading it just now, could easily have recited the poem from memory.

At a time when Swami was living in Italy, he fell gravely ill and had to be hospitalized. He remarked to me how uplifted he felt by the purity and innocence of an eighty-year-old nun who would come into his room to perform some simple tasks. He said that he could feel her dedication and devotion to the renunciate life and to God, and that he felt greatly healed by her spirit.

When I took the assignment to manage Swami's special projects, I found that this included his publications. At that point his publishing department had changed its name three times in as many years. The name when I took it over was Joyful Arts Production Association (JAPA). It was a nice enough name, but it didn't actually tell bookstores, other publishers, and book buyers about the kind of books we published.

In the late 1970s, Swami had written a thin booklet called *Meaning in the Arts*. Now, years later, when he expanded it into a book, he received the inspiration for a new title, *Crystal Clarity in the Arts*. He wrote a definition for Crystal Clarity, which stirred much interest amongst his readers. Since we had been searching for a new name for the publishing department, a light went on in my brain: It would be a wonderful name for the publishing department! It speaks to an expansive awareness of all those with whom we interact.

I decided to experiment with creating a very large poster with Swami's definition printed prominently on it. I brought it to the

American and the international publishing trade shows and displayed it in our stands. I was amazed by the hundreds of people who would stop and read it carefully, then step inside to see what our books were about.

When I asked for Swami's approval of this new name, he readily agreed. We would be known as Crystal Clarity, Publishers, reflecting the expansive consciousness at the heart of his books, talks, and musical compositions.

Swami's definition of Crystal Clarity:

> To live in Crystal Clarity means to see oneself, and all things, as aspects of a greater reality; to seek to enter into conscious attunement with that reality; and to see all things as channels for the expression of that reality.
>
> It means to see truth in simplicity; to seek always to be guided by the simple truth, not by opinion; and by what IS, not by one's own desires or prejudices.
>
> It means striving to see things in relation to their broadest potential.
>
> In one's association with other people, it means seeking always to include their realities in one's own.

※

About a year after we'd taken the name Crystal Clarity, I met Swami in his garden, where he was sitting at the table there, writing. In that peaceful setting, he said, "Someone mentioned to me that we should consider changing our publishing name to ———." I don't recall the name, probably because I "saw red" before he'd even completed the sentence! I immediately launched in about why it was a terrible idea to change our name yet again. At one point in my torrential verbal outpouring, I glanced at Swami: He was completely calm, simply looking at me until I finished my rant. In the mirror of his eyes, I saw my lips flapping with way too many words. He wasn't judging me; he was, simply, calmly attentive—and I was *not*! He didn't say anything further, except to agree that we wouldn't change the name again. *Lesson learned: Banish restlessness. Stay calm. Slow down the reactive process.* Where would I be without meditation? And how far did I still have to travel?

༄

In his book *Education for Life*, Swami defines maturity as the ability to relate to realities other than one's own. I learned an interesting lesson from him in this regard. One time I told him that someone had requested we handle a project a certain way, and I was concerned that it wouldn't help him spiritually to acquiesce to the request.

Swami's response was interesting. He said, "When someone requests something, it is important to consider both what it means to him, and what it means to us." His point was that even though we might not think it best for him, the fact that he had asked suggested that he might well benefit by being given the opportunity to give it a try and learn in the process. In fact, Swami continued, it could also be helpful for us to bend in his direction. "If necessary," he added, "we should bend some more, and then bend even more, as far as we can, but just short of snapping."

I took it as invaluable guidance on how to relate to realities other than our own: to behave with true maturity, by acknowledging that there can be more than one way to do a thing, and to be flexible with others' approaches, allowing them to learn from their experiences.

༶

I received the following note from Swami on Thanksgiving Day 2012, his last Thanksgiving on this earthly plane. I found his comments on Thanksgiving, and on the latter years of our lives, very interesting:

> We had a lovely Thanksgiving lunch here. I'd love to see this holiday recognized everywhere!
>
> My old age doesn't seem to be giving me any rest. But I said to a few friends yesterday that I don't want this to be the pattern for all community members' lives. I strongly believe the best thing is to spend one's last years in seclusion and meditation. If God hasn't given me that, He is making up for it in other ways!
>
> Love to you both, and to everyone there,
>
> swami

My thoughts:

For those active in Yogananda's work and the broader communities movement, these thoughts are well worth considering and preserving. We are still in the pioneering phase of this work. Many of us who belong to the first and second generations can see no hope for years of seclusion at the end of our lives, which we expect will continue to be busy with active outward service. Still, what an incredible gift it will be—both for themselves and for the whole world—for those of us who can spend the latter years of their lives in seclusion and meditation. The ripples of peace they create by meditating deeply will surely spread far and be a tangible blessing for all.

Swami's friendship was impersonal. "No one," he would say, "is special to me. I love everyone equally."

He was reminding us that those who were often together with him were no more special to him than others whom he hardly ever saw. His friendship was impersonal, and if we related to him in that manner, we found that our interactions were harmonious, and fulfilling. But if we became too personally attached to him, we would find ourselves not hearing from him until that attitude had shifted. Non-attachment was at the heart of the true friendship that he held out to us all.

When we began giving Sunday services at the original community, I had to overcome a degree of nervousness. Early on, my husband and I gave a service on Palm Sunday. Swami rarely attended the services in those days, as he was deeply engaged with writing projects or composing music. But on this Sunday, he walked in just before we began—and sat in the front row! I was petrified; but what could I do?

Then the most amazing thing happened: I felt incredibly supported. Instead of feeling from Swami the all-too-common human tendency to evaluate and judge, I experienced only his unconditional love and support. Swami helped me that morning to let go of all my attachments and fears, and love and strength rushed in to fill the void.

Swami taught me about balance, and being natural and genuine. After we gave our first Sunday service at the original community, he invited us to his home for tea. When we entered, I heard familiar music wafting through his apartment. It was familiar because I had listened to it throughout my childhood—it was my father's favorite music, by Benny Goodman. I was surprised and delighted! Surprised, that Swami was listening to that music, and by the realization that he had been a young man in the same era as my father.

And delighted that he was so natural in himself. He wasn't trying to be anyone other than who he was. Benny Goodman was hardly a significant part of his life, but now and then he felt inwardly free to listen to a variety of music that he enjoyed.

That said, for public gatherings at his communities we always played music that Swami or Yogananda had composed. This music is infused with the vibrations of the higher consciousness from which it had been received, and of Yogananda's path specifically. Even without a lecture or program, simply by listening to this music one experiences expansion and attunement.

When Swami had surgery for a cancerous tumor at age eighty, he insisted on leaving the hospital much sooner than the doctors preferred. It was Swami's habitual preference, however, whenever he was hospitalized—which was often.

Swami's home in Gurgaon, a suburb of New Delhi, India, had several stories; his bedroom was on the second floor. When he arrived from the hospital, he leaned on several friends as he came through the front door. We sat him down on the first comfortable couch, at the base of the stairs. He graciously sat and chatted with us for a few minutes and took some refreshments, although he was clearly exhausted and out of breath. We assumed that he would need to be carried up the stairs, given how weak he appeared. Then, in a flash, he announced that it was time to head up to his bedroom, and began making his way to the staircase on his own.

We could clearly see blood from his surgical wound seeping through his clothing, but by the same time we noticed, he had begun walking up the stairs. The men instantly leapt into action, but he motioned them away. What began with "walking" suddenly became bolting upstairs like a gazelle! God had literally put a bounce in his step—and if we hadn't seen it with our own eyes, we wouldn't have believed it.

Swami was completely non-attached to his body. And he had great inner strength, gained through many lives of meditation, yoga, and attunement with his guru.

※

Once, we were vacationing with Swami and another couple in Taormina, a picturesque resort on the east coast of Sicily, on the Ionian Sea. Throughout the vacation it seemed that I could do nothing right. A constant flow of corrections came my way. After several days, I found myself alone with Swami at a restaurant, waiting for the others to join us. At one point, he related a story from Yogananda's youth in the ashram of his guru, Sri Yukteswar. While serving a tray of tea to the guests, Yogananda tripped on the rug, whereupon the Guru laughed heartily and pointed out his clumsiness to the assembled visitors. Yogananda passed the test by taking the correction calmly.

Swami said nothing further as the conversation moved to other subjects. I realized that he had been giving me the opportunity to respond calmly to the flurry of corrections on this vacation. This allowed my heart to settle in gratitude. Yet another lesson in non-attachment and expansion!

During a seclusion near Assisi, Italy, Swami received the inspiration for a ceremony called the "Festival of Light," which we led at the end of our Sunday services. As part of the ceremony, there is a "blessing of light from the Masters." The Lightbearer touches each person at the point between the eyebrows, the seat of God-consciousness in the human body.

Swami explained to the Lightbearers that the touch of light was meant to be only a "touch," not a long, drawn-out blessing, and that they should remain impersonal, not looking the person in the eyes or smiling, but remaining focused inwardly.

The Festival of Light is meant to bring us more and more within, so that by the conclusion we can have an experience of divine joy, which is calm, non-attached, and internalized.

When Swami was nine years old, his parents enrolled him in a boarding school in Switzerland, where his doctors believed the climate would help him recover from a long, painful bout of colitis. When I asked him if being separated from his parents at such a young age had been difficult, or if he had enjoyed being independent from them, he replied that he had been too young to be sent away, and that it had been very difficult. That struck me, for in all the years I'd known him, Swami was strongly independent by nature. As a new parent, I found his response helpful, especially since our son was extremely independent. Even children like that, however, need nurturing love and affection.

Some years, Swami would join our publishing team at the annual United States publishing trade show. A prolific composer, he usually had an album that had recently been released. And as one who loved to buy the latest audio devices, he would bring along a portable cassette player and place the headphones over the ears of an unsuspecting prospective buyer as he was passing by, so that he could enjoy one of Swami's latest compositions. Invariably, the buyer would be delighted, and would become engaged in enthusiastic conversation with Swami. Swami would sometimes burst into song, to give him a live experience of the piece, saturated with his vibrations. The lesson: *Don't be shy about sharing a good thing that you believe in, or concerned with what people might think.*

In the early years of the first community, things were quite rustic. Our homes had no electricity, phones, or indoor plumbing. And the roads were unpaved, so there was lots of mud in winter and dust in summer. One might say that our clothing, too, was strictly rustic. It appeared as if we were "wearing our renunciation on our sleeves."

Swami always carried himself with dignity and dressed in refined but simple good taste when he was in public. A group of us were vacationing with him in Carmel, a beautiful resort town on the coast, a hundred miles south of San Francisco. Carmel is known for its lovely shops. When we entered a clothing store together, Swami insisted that one of the ladies try on a simple dress he had selected for her. She looked transformed! He then remarked that renunciation is *not* synonymous with shabby or tattered clothing. On the contrary, clean, attractive clothing, far from expressing worldliness, demonstrates our respect for our bodily temples, and for others.

St. Francis had his followers take vows of poverty. Swami explained that in this age, spirituality is best defined instead by simplicity. Simplicity he defined as "reducing one's wants so that material things do not intrude on one's inner freedom, but rather, in the context of whatever needs to be done, facilitate that freedom."

The vows of the Franciscan Order were (and still are) "poverty, chastity, and obedience." Those vows' counterparts today, in

Yogananda's teachings, are simplicity, moderation, and cooperative obedience. The last means obedience which involves the cooperation of both parties, rather than one enforcing its will over another.

❧

After Swami's cancer surgery, several of us stayed with him in his hospital suite in Delhi. I call it a "suite" because it was the largest hospital room I had ever seen—it included a sitting room, bedroom, and private bathroom. Swami was in an especially blissful state. When one of the other ladies and I were arranging his bed, he said, "When you were both young, I saw your beauty, but now I only see the beauty of your souls." The truth is that Swami always related only to a person's soul. He only ever saw the highest in us. He had always been in that expanded state.

❧

Swami believed that a third person should be present when ministers and teachers had private interviews or consultations with someone of the opposite gender. This simple principle promotes an atmosphere of respectful non-attachment.

❧

Sometime around 1988, I met a minister from Self-Realization Fellowship (the organization Paramhansa Yogananda founded in this country for the dissemination of his teachings) who told me that Yogananda had a "blueprint" for the future of his work. When I mentioned the conversation to Swami, he said, "Not so. Yogananda always responded to decisions in the moment, asking Divine Mother inwardly for guidance. Besides," he continued, "if there had been a blueprint, then why was I made the Vice-President of SRF? Wouldn't they have seen from the blueprint that they would kick me out?"

In the spiritual life, there can never be a fixed, inflexible "blueprint." God is expansive and doesn't have a preordained master plan for how the universe will unfold.

In 2009, Swami received the inspiration to create a new renunciate order. He called it the Nayaswami Order, meaning the "New Swami" Order. Those who take the final vow are called nayaswamis. Soon, there was an ordination ceremony at which a number of us took the nayaswami vows. Others took preliminary vows of renunciation: brahmacharya if they were single with no plans to marry; tyaga if they were married and without young, dependent children. And still others, not as yet ready to take renunciate vows, but wishing to direct their lives to living for God, took the "pilgrim" vow.

In January 2010, Swami explained in a letter to some of us why he continued to sign his name "Swami" instead of "Nayaswami." He said that we should feel free to do the same, because we *are* swamis: *new* (*naya*) swamis. Also, it is awkward for people to address us as "Nayaswami." He asked for our opinions.

There are two takeaways from this. First, even if he had a clear stand on a matter, he would invite our ideas, to see (as he put it) if there were aspects that he hadn't considered. In this case, I believe he wanted to make it clear that the Nayaswami Order was a continuation of the Swami Order founded in the ninth century by the great sage Adi Shankaracharya. The term *naya* is added to signify a new expression of the spirit of renunciation embodied in the ancient spiritual tradition of India, one appropriate to the current times, and reaching toward the future. Appropriate for an age when the monastery walls have fallen, and the world's consciousness has become sufficiently refined to allow an emphasis, not on all the things one isn't supposed to do, but rather on that to which all truly aspire: ego-transcendence, that is, rather than ego-suppression. An age, also, in which aspirants from pilgrims to nayaswamis, should they choose to live together in spiritual communities, can do so with less risk to their inner calling than in the age of materialism.

※

In the final stage of her life, Kamala Silva, a close, direct disciple of Yogananda's, came to live at the original community. She suffered from dementia, and needed constant companionship and care. Several of us took turns helping attend to her needs. Kamala remembered none of the people and events in her life, but if we mentioned Yogananda's name she would immediately light up and recall many of her encounters with him. Once, after spending time with her, I saw Swami and asked him, "She was such a high soul spiritually. How can she be facing dementia?" "Padma," he replied, "we are not our bodies, and we are not our *minds*, either!" We limit ourselves to our bodies and minds, when in reality we are sparks of the infinite consciousness.

※

Once, when I was visiting Swami in India, he took a few of us to dinner at the Trident Hotel. It was glorious! After dinner, we walked past the hotel's very upscale gift shop. When Swami went in, I held my breath.

It was very expensive—I was mentally holding on tightly to my wallet. Then Swami said, "You should purchase something, Padma." Oh my, I couldn't get out of it now! I looked carefully at the items: everything was beautiful. Finally, my eyes landed on a tiny silver picture frame. It was lovely: the oval frame was fashioned in a classical Indian pattern. And it was the least expensive item I could find.

Swami was pleased with my selection. I could tell by the twinkle in his eye that he had been testing me. He was still trying to help me to release my thrifty roots, and to understand that true renunciation resides within. As soon as we arrived back home, I placed a small portrait of him in the frame. To this day it adorns my meditation space, along with the precious memory of the lesson that accompanied it.

Swami had a repertoire of movies that he enjoyed watching repeatedly. In fact, if you recommended a new one to him, you had to be prepared for him to turn it off after a few minutes. The movies he loved were either sensitively spiritual, or ones in which the characters had good hearts. A comedy occasionally made his list, including several films with Danny Kaye.

Toward the end of his life, I remember watching a movie with him about St. Bernadette of Lourdes. We had watched it many times before. The room was dark, but when I glanced at him, I saw tears streaming down his cheeks. He was moved deeply by her renunciation and sanctity. No words. Just blissful.

Chapter Ten

Ego-Transcendence

WHEN I WAS still new in the community, I was invited to a satsang (gathering) at Swami's home. After a brief talk, he invited our questions.

I asked, "Is all fear rooted in the fear of death?" He replied, "No. All fear is rooted in ego."

His answer made complete sense to me. It's the ego that is afraid of dying, and that fears anything that might diminish its dominion. Ego holds us hostage. Hence, all true spiritual traditions teach that if we want to enjoy increasing inner happiness and freedom, we must transcend the ego's desires.

When I managed the publishing department, we had someone who ran the printing press, and a sales staff, but no writers. At one point, Swami needed back cover copy for the book he'd just written. He would often write the cover copy himself, but on this occasion he asked me to help, as he was already busily at work on his next book. When I replied, "But I'm not a writer!" he exclaimed, "Don't ever say that!" He added, "You can do anything you put your mind to!"

The ego says, "I'm this"—"I'm that." But God is within everyone, and He can do *anything* through us.

Swami told us that Yogananda advised the monastics in his ashram not to waste their time playing chess. He encouraged them to spend as much time as possible in meditation.

Yogananda would occasionally take the monastics with him to the movies, or on vacation to Yosemite, or on picnics, or for ice cream. He didn't discourage wholesome, relaxing activities, only card and board games and reading too many novels.

In our ego-selves we cling to the people, objects, and activities that please us. "It's a free country—I can pursue any hobbies I want!" But in the spiritual life, and in particular the monastic life, our goal is to transcend the ego. It's a steep ascent up a high mountain. It is said that Yogananda read only one novel to the end: *The Life Everlasting*, by Marie Corelli.

I recall a time when the publishing sales reached the stars, with more than double compared to any prior year. I was thrilled to report the news to Swami. "That is wonderful," he replied. "Let's try to double that next year!" I remember the exact moment, including the spot where we were standing—and the deflation I felt as my heart sank, and I lowered my head to gaze to the ground.

Noticing my downcast demeanor, Swami asked, "What's wrong?"
"Sir," I responded, "it seems as if it's never enough!" The moment those words left my lips, I understood that until we are free in God, it really *is* "never enough." Even when we feel we're taking giant leaps in the right direction, there's always something more to aspire to, until we are able to merge forever in the bliss of God. When someone asked Yogananda, "Does spiritual progress have an end?" he replied, "No end. You go on until you achieve endlessness."

Of course, we aren't reaching outside ourselves: Transcending the ego is more like peeling away the layers of an onion until we reach the transparent center.

Someone in our Sangha lay dying; my husband and I were asked to go and support him. We asked Swami for his counsel, and this is what he offered. "Chant AUM in his right ear. Place your index finger on his spiritual eye to help coax the life force toward that point. When possible, at the moment of passing, chant the Gayatri Mantra."

Swami suggested to ministers and teachers: Don't tell stories about how good you are, or how well you did something. Instead, tell stories about your mistakes, and how you learned from them.

When Swami finished writing the book *Education for Life*, he asked some of us to go out and promote it. At one point, we arranged public talks for him in the nearby small town of Nevada City, and in Sacramento, the state capital.

Swami had an idea for getting parents' attention: We would create a flyer with the provocative headline, "Why Is Johnny Angry?" It was 1986, a time when many teens and even younger children were expressing their anger through drug use and chaotic behavior. It was a new fact of life for parents and teachers.

When the flyers were printed, we stood in front of supermarkets and handed them to the passing shoppers. This task was a spiritual test: a test of humility, and of letting go of our attachment to what others might think of us.

This exercise gave me an appreciation for the art of creatively capturing people's attention. I've tried to keep someone on staff who could think outside the box when writing headlines. If we weren't able to achieve the necessary creativity, we would look for someone in another department who could help.

I had a dream in which my husband and I were standing with Swami as he was about to go on stage to address a large audience. He was talking with the man who would lead the audience in chanting, and said, "Please remember that although you have power and magnetism, you need to let God's vibration catch up to you, otherwise your power will be used in the wrong way."

When speaking or chanting in public, it's easy to allow the talk or music to carry us. But we need to remember—lest we fall into the insidious trap of the ego—to invite God to speak and sing through us.

Swami urged us not to give unsolicited advice. It's too easy to fall in love with the sound of our own voice, and fail to hear what the other person is actually saying or meaning. Swami taught us to listen carefully, then ask questions that would help people arrive at their own conclusions.

In the last few years of his life, Swami said to a number of those close to him, "I can see where on the spectrum between the medulla and the spiritual eye your ego resides." In the teachings of India, the medulla, at the top of the spine and at the base of the skull, is the negative pole of the spiritual eye; they are opposite parts of the same chakra. The medulla is the seat of the ego, and the spiritual eye is the seat of the soul. Swami was saying that he could see how much we were influenced by (rooted in) ego, and how much we had been magnetized toward our true soul nature.

Swami encouraged us, as Yogananda had encouraged him, to try to live with our attention always calmly focused at the spiritual eye. The more we do so, he explained, the more uplifted we will be, the less the ego will be able to pull us down, and the more rapid will be our spiritual progress.

☙

When Swami ordained my husband and me as Lightbearers, he did something that I had never seen him do before, nor have I seen him do it since. With his right hand, he placed his index finger on my spiritual eye, and with his left hand he placed his index finger at the medulla. Then he rotated the finger on the medulla, as if to loosen the ego and release it forward to the spiritual eye.

☙

Swami was the embodiment of living superconsciously. To live superconsciously means to see all life as unitive: to live in a consciousness of unity rather than separation, and intuitively rather than analytically. One who lives superconsciously perseveres until solutions are found.

Here are two passages from a letter Yogananda wrote to Swami, as part of his training of him to live superconsciously. I reproduce his words exactly as he handwrote them.

Get up early, meditate a little, exercise and run or walk briskly; then start from 8 A.M. to 6 P.M. Every two hours run for 5 minutes and meditate 15 minutes before lunch—including lunch must be finished in 1 hour. Work—9 hours a day with deep concentration—meditate two hours deeply at night after dining at 6:30. Sleep 7 hours. Be sure to walk briskly or run for 5 minutes every 2 hours. This will keep strain out. After dinner at night walk on the road and not in jungly brush—for one hour 6 to 7. Then eat and meditate two hours. Adjust routine whatever possible. Not necessary to walk at night. You can work from 7:30 A.M.—if you like. You should take ½ hours walk in the morning after quick meditation and breakfast covering (½ hour).

. . .

Q. How much have you edited? <u>Thorough</u> but <u>fast</u> editing is necessary, or nothing will be done. Time is scant.

With blessing,

P Yogananda

P.S. Do all work with the thought of God. PY

Most of us imagine that we are directing our own lives. I find it interesting to see the level of detail that Yogananda devoted to guiding Swami's life. Because his advice came from the consciousness of a fully Self-realized master, it shows us that God wants to guide *all* of our thoughts and actions, even the most fleeting and seemingly insignificant! The ego may feel hemmed in, but the soul feels free in living at the center of God's will.

Swami took his monastic vows from Master at their first meeting, on September 12, 1948. He took his final vows as a swami in 1955, and for the rest of his life he lived in the consciousness of a renunciate.

He founded the first community in 1969. By the early 1980s many of the married couples had begun to feel like spiritually second-class citizens compared to the monks and nuns. In 1985 Swami married an Italian devotee, Rosanna Golia, whom he had met in Italy. Rosanna and Swami lived together for several years at the original community in California. The marriage helped us understand the value and noble calling of both paths.

Most of the community embraced these changes, but it was controversial for some, and they moved away. After about five years, the marriage fell apart, and they divorced.

After some difficult years leading up to the divorce, Swami decided to go to India for seclusion. When he came out, Swami called to tell me that he had prayed deeply, and decided that he still felt a strong monastic calling. His love for God, and his desire to transcend the ego, were still uppermost for him. At his altar during the seclusion, he had resumed his monastic vows.

Serving as manager of the publishing department sometimes felt like herding wild horses! One day, two of the men announced a plan that would require Swami to write a few specific books on topics which their research had shown them to be marketable.

I was far from enthusiastic, because I knew that Swami wrote only as God inspired him. He never chose topics based on their possible market value. When I asked the men to speak to Swami about their idea, they hesitated, because they believed the plan would stand a better chance if I suggested it. So I compromised: I agreed to go to the meeting, but they would have to present their ideas.

When we arrived at Swami's apartment, they sat directly across from him, while I sat to the side. They proceeded to present their ideas, including the research, while Swami listened quietly.

When they had finished, Swami turned in my direction and began to scold *me*! "You know I don't work that way," he said. "How presumptuous to think that I would write these books, as if I ever write 'for the market.' You know I write as God inspires me to write." The scolding seemed to last an eternity, and all the while he was looking at me. When he finished, the men scurried out, and I followed.

Swami's scolding shook me to my core. I understood that, as the person in charge, I was responsible for deciding all matters concerning our publishing plans. Swami was someone one wished to please, and to feel his displeasure was painful. I tried my best to absorb the blow, but I felt as though my spine were reverberating, and hollow.

For two days I remained shaken. I desperately tried to give myself to God in meditation, but I didn't get far! Then, Swami called and said, "I wanted them to hear what I had to say, but I knew they couldn't take it, and I knew that you *could* take it."

It was a profound lesson, and one that has always remained with me: to trust my understanding of a situation, and follow my intuition, while at the same time letting the ego rattle around inside, however it might. Ego needs a good shaking now and then!

༄

During a period of severe testing, Swami was asked if it was due to bad karma. He replied that any situation we face is either a result of karma, or is due to *tapasya*.

Tapasya is a Sanskrit word meaning "sacrifice." It involves raising our energy to meet life's pains and challenges with calm acceptance. Through this process the ego is purified. On the road to Self-realization, such purification is a necessity for everyone. I understood Swami's answer to mean that some tests come due to our self-created karma, while others are to help us raise our energy above the test, and, in overcoming it, to become stronger in ourselves.

Chapter Eleven

Intuition and Attunement

Years ago, Swami invited us to vacation with him and two other couples at Sirmione, on Lago di Garda, not far from Venice. Swami was in the habit of taking an afternoon nap, and often then writing late into the night. One afternoon while he was napping, my husband Hriman and I strolled through the cobblestone streets of the picturesque village. We came across a men's clothing store that had a sweater on a mannequin in the window. I immediately thought that it would look great on Hriman. But, sure enough, his stubborn thrifty Irish side got the better of him, and he declined to try it on. "I don't need another sweater," he protested. We continued our walk and returned to the hotel without seeing any of our friends.

At the appointed time, we met Swami and the others for afternoon tea at the hotel's cafe. Afterward, we took our daily "after-tea" stroll to the village. A few feet past that same men's shop, Swami turned back and said, "Hriman, that sweater would look really nice on you. Let's go in so you can try it on."

Hriman had a puzzled look on his face. He knew that Swami had been asleep when we went by this shop earlier, and that since I had been with him the entire time, I couldn't possibly have told Swami about it.

Reluctantly, Hriman tried on the sweater amid protestations: "I don't need a sweater, and I can't afford it." Of course, the sweater looked just right on him, and Swami promptly purchased it for him. Swami had encouraged Hriman and me to be more flexible in the way we thought about financial matters. The sweater remains a beautiful reminder of his encouragement, and of his kindness.

"My thoughts are not your thoughts, neither are your ways my ways, saith the Lord." This Bible verse captures how we often saw Swami's ways. He was utterly unpredictable! Earlier I mentioned the large, luxury mansion we leased in San Francisco—at a time when, back at the first community, we barely even had electricity!

Then there was the check for $10,000 that he sent to the nun in the Philippines in response to her plea, though he had never heard of her before that day.

Here is another example. Swami loved bookstores. He saw them, he once mentioned to me, as repositories of ideas. Whenever he visited his parents in Atherton, California, he enjoyed visiting the East West Bookshop a few blocks away in Menlo Park.

One day, the owner (by now they were on a first-name basis) said she was needing to sell the store, and asked if Swami would like to purchase it. He checked inwardly, and promptly said "YES!" The down payment was a large sum which we didn't have, but a donation for that amount was miraculously received, and soon after the right managers were found.

Swami wouldn't have made such an important decision based on his reason alone. He always sought his guru's guidance inwardly, and if he felt it was the right thing, the necessary funds and people had a way of miraculously appearing. East West grew to become one of the most prominent New Thought bookstores in the entire country. Now, over forty years later, at a time when many bookstores have been forced to close, it continues to operate successfully, as does a sister store of the same name that we opened later in Seattle.

After my home was destroyed in the fire of 1976, we lived for a while in the nearby town of Nevada City. Once the construction of our new home in the community was underway, friends began encouraging us to move back before it was completed, because the community's workload was piling up. So I asked Swami one day what he thought about our returning sooner. He replied, "God doesn't care *where* we live. God cares *how* we live."

Since I was first introduced to *Autobiography of a Yogi* by Paramhansa Yogananda in 1970, I have reread it often, and each time I've discovered new teachings and subtle meanings. Many others have reported the same experience.

About twenty-five years before Swami left his body, I noticed that the words to one of Yogananda's chants appeared in the book, and I realized that there was a word in the chant that many people (but not Swami) had begun to sing differently.

I was managing Swami's publications department at the time, and I pointed it out to him. He replied that changes will often creep in for no apparent reason, and he asked me to let the music department know so that they could lead people in singing it the way Yogananda had intended.

Here are Yogananda's words as they appear in *Cosmic Chants* (the book of his chants compiled by his organization), but including the above correction:

Where Is There Love?

In this world, Mother, no one can love me.
In this world they do not know how to love me.
In this world, Mother, no one can love me.
In this world they do not know how to love me.
Where is there pure loving love?
Where is there truly loving Thee?*
There my soul longs to be. There my soul longs to be.

When I worked in publishing in the original community, my office was near Swami's residence. Almost daily, he would invite

---

* Instead of "Thee," people were singing "me." This gave it an altogether different meaning!

me over at five in the afternoon for tea, when he would ask for updates on the sales and progress of his books. I attended many other meetings at his home as well.

Whenever I walked to Swami's, and as I approached his building, it was as if I were entering an astral cloud. I could suddenly no longer think linearly; I could only experience things intuitively. I would often muse about the experience. Although it took me out of my comfort zone, I looked forward to it with delighted anticipation. It was a completely different way of relating that I hadn't experienced before, nor have I had the same experience since.

After we'd moved to Seattle, Swami would send us perhaps twenty pages from his current writing project, then he would call twenty minutes later to ask for our feedback. This happened constantly. For a long time it puzzled me, since he had given Hriman and me such a big job to do in the Washington community. It seemed he expected us to drop everything and read his manuscript instead.

In time, I understood that attunement to the highest reality should be our constant priority, and that reading his manuscript would help greatly in that regard. There would always be time to complete our other duties. It wasn't unlike the Bible story of Martha and Mary. Martha, who was busy serving the guests, became upset with Mary for not helping her. Meanwhile, Mary sat at Jesus' feet, absorbing his wisdom and his vibrations. Jesus explained that Mary had "chosen that better part," because attunement to his divine consciousness was, by far, her highest duty.

There was a second lesson here, regarding delegation. Swami constantly emphasized the need to delegate tasks. Often, we become so attached to our duties that we're quite sure no one could do them as well or efficiently as we can. He wanted us to understand that in delegating tasks to others, we empower them to develop their creativity and attunement. Perhaps they will complete the tasks in new and innovative ways. By handing off those tasks, we also magically free up time and energy to develop our own attunement by serving in creative new ways.

❧

I was at a restaurant with Swami and a few other friends. Whenever we were around him, we were on our best behavior. It wasn't a pretense—the reality is that it was difficult to be around him and harbor critical or negative thoughts about ourselves or others. When we'd ordered, Swami excused himself to find the restroom.

When he left the table, the conversation immediately shifted. We began talking about someone who was difficult to get along with, and the ways we'd found to cope with him. When Swami reappeared, he completed the last sentence that one of us was in the midst of finishing. We were stunned! It seemed there was a remote device that was wired to his hearing aid, and he had accidentally left it on the table! Thus he had heard the entire discussion. It was a stark reminder that we should always behave as if God is present, because God *is* always watching us (and listening)!

Intuition and Attunement

Swami had met his guru on a Sunday. When we asked Swami to marry us, he said, "A Sunday would be nice." Sunday is a sacred day, when our consciousness is uplifted. Swami rarely spelled things out for us; he simply offered his gentle suggestions. "A Sunday would be nice."

Swami was discussing Yogananda's healing techniques with several of us, and telling us how they differ from other methods. He explained that most other healing systems draw on the teachings of masters of other traditions. What distinguishes Yogananda's techniques is that they use *willpower* to focus energy, and of course that they draw on Yogananda himself. Swami encouraged us to develop Yogananda's system, so that after completing a course of study one could receive a certificate as a practitioner of Yogananda's healing techniques.

"Fulfill your word in Truth." I was always keenly aware that Swami was a man of his word. Once that was given, he would allow nothing to prevent him from honoring it. I remember a poignant example when we were with him one time in Assisi. Swami would often purchase his newspaper from a small vendor near the Portiuncula, the tiny church that St. Francis had built. One day, we went with him to the Portiuncula to meditate. He had other errands to run, so after meditating he stopped at the vendor's stall and told him that he would be back later for his newspaper. By the time he had completed his errands, we were on the other side of town, yet Swami drove all the way back to that vendor, simply to keep his word.

Patanjali, in his Yoga Sutras, speaks of the importance of being truthful in all things. A practice such as Swami's, of always keeping one's word, helps us realize that when we are in alignment with Truth, we are attuning ourselves with the God who is present in our soul.

When I first started working on Swami's special projects, he began handing me his manuscripts to publish, although I had zero experience with publishing! I researched the various ways in which books are paginated, and then I asked Swami how he wanted his books done. His replied, "Look at *Autobiography of a Yogi*: That is how I want all my books to be paginated, please."

Yogananda was Swami's constant touchstone for deciding every detail of his life. Attunement with a saint is not a mental abstraction or a superficial sentiment. It means literally walking in his footsteps in both small and large ways.

I was enjoying a seemingly casual conversation with Swami, but it turned out to offer an important truth. I told him that someone had asked me if we needed the guru's physical touch to be freed in God. Swami responded: "Master did say that the scriptures of India say that. However, he also asked me to give people initiation, even while he was alive. In other words, God works through disciples." Swami continued in that vein, then concluded by saying, "Don't accept things at face value, not even things Master said. Try to understand them from the inside. Ask yourself questions about it. Win yourself over with sweet reason."

When we learn to read, we're also taught comprehension. Being able to state a Master's teaching isn't enough. We need to understand the teaching in order to *live* it! In time, understanding brings us to attunement.

After I'd served for a time at the community in Washington state, someone asked me to join her for a complimentary haircut by the man who cut her own hair. He worked in a trendy upscale salon near downtown Seattle, and cut my hair in a new way that made me look quite different. I received lots of compliments on my new "style."

The next day, I left for a series of meetings with Swami in California. When Swami walked into the room, he said, "What did you do to your hair? You don't look like the Padma we know and love." Swami had never commented on my hair, but I understood the message: My trendy new haircut might be admired by the world, but it was not fitting to my spiritual life. It drew attention to me, rather than to my inner Self. I never returned to the "hip" salon.

❧

Swami asked us not to put his picture on any public altars. He never held himself out as a master, and pointed everyone to Yogananda in that regard.

❧

At a time when we were extremely busy facilitating the building of the Blue Lotus Temple in Seattle and launching new programs to be offered there, one morning found me working a few hours from home when Swami called. I was thrilled to hear his voice, and I told him so. To my surprise, he said, "What do you mean? I've been calling you many times, but you never answer."

At the time, cell phones were starting to be the norm, and it was only years later that I realized I could have forwarded our home phone to my cell. I'm sharing this story because I realized that I could have done more to be available to speak with Swami, but in my "busyness," my mind was not still enough to receive solutions.

It was never personal with Swami. He was trying to help me, and I simply let myself get too busy to recognize an opportunity to receive his assistance. In this way, we may also find ourselves "too busy" to be available to God. Stay alert, or as Yogananda used to say, "Awake and ready!"

❧

I was feeling that a certain couple were struggling in their marriage. When I mentioned it to Swami, he immediately picked up the phone and called them. The wife answered, and he spoke with her briefly, then asked to speak with the husband. After a few moments, he signed off. He turned to me and said, "They are fine." He had listened sensitively to their voices, and he knew that they were, or would be, all right.

Swami often said that we project vibrations through the voice. The ability to pick up on them is not one that was unique to him; it is universal. When we learn to still the mind in meditation, we become more sensitive and intuitive in this regard. This example prompted me to listen more sensitively to the tone and vibrations of people's voices, and to test my intuition regarding their meaning and intentions.

※

In the early 1950s, Yogananda asked Swami to come with him to his desert retreat, where he was dictating his commentaries on the Bhagavad Gita. It was his intention to have Swami and another disciple work on editing them in preparation for publication.

However, the book wasn't published during Swami's years in SRF, and the organization retained the manuscript, to which he no longer had access.

Swami's handwritten edits were in the margins. For decades he brainstormed how he could get hold of the manuscript. Then, in

2006—he was living in Gurgaon, India, at the time—he became discouraged at the thought that he might never be able to complete the task his guru had given him. One night he had a dream in which Yogananda said, "Don't overlook the possibility of a skylight." He added, "A sense of adventure is needed."

Swami immediately sat down to write Yogananda's commentaries from memory. That was the skylight: Yogananda flooded his brain with memories of what he'd dictated all those years ago. Swami was thrilled: The Master's bliss flooded his being. Swami explained that although he might not have remembered each word exactly, he recalled the feeling of Yogananda's words and meaning.

During this period we had the blessing of visiting Swami for two weeks. He would come bounding downstairs with the latest ten pages, thrilled by their depth of inspiration. He would sit and read them with us, as if for the first time, and as if in writing them he had been merely a humble witness. The pages flowed through him like a bounding river. To this day, I believe it is the best book Swami ever wrote. The one-pointed attunement he experienced with his guru is tangible in it.

My mother tongue is Dutch—our family came to the U.S. when I was in fifth grade. Swami would have fun with me by deliberately mispronouncing the painter Vincent Van Gogh's name, then he would wait for me to correct him. This happened dozens of times! It was only years after his passing that a clear intuition came to me: that Swami had been trying to break me of the habit of correcting people, that I might concentrate on offering them inspiration instead.

❧

A woman who was unknown to us brought a dessert for Swami, prepared by her spiritual teacher, at a time when he wasn't at home. His staff put it in his refrigerator, and when he returned, he found it and enjoyed it greatly. He told us that it had been made by a saintly soul, and that her vibrations were astral in their purity.

Swami could tell when a dish had been prepared by a person of elevated consciousness. He told us that anyone can develop a similar intuitive ability by learning to become sufficiently still in heart and mind to receive it. Intuition is of the heart rather than the intellect. To develop it doesn't mean that we should become emotionally engaged with our feelings, in the way that can lead to being overly sensitive or easily hurt. Intuition is calm feeling. It is the only truly reliable way of *knowing*.

❧

When Swami had hip replacement surgery, I was part of a rotation of devotees who cared for him. On one occasion, not wanting to awaken him needlessly, I gently opened the door to his room. I found him sitting on the edge of the bed with his back to me, doing what he could of Yogananda's energization exercises. He didn't know I was there. It was another of so many examples showing how he followed his guru's prescription to practice the techniques; and when it is not possible to do them fully, then to do whatever we can do in an utmost effort at *attunement*! God watches the heart.

❧

To help us learn to use our intuition, Swami would rarely spell things out for us. It was a way of teaching that Yogananda too had practiced with his disciples.

At one point, Swami wrote four small books for children. When a teacher in the school commented that the books would be "over the heads" of most children, Swami replied that it was important for children to "reach for understanding" in order to develop their intuition. We all (children included) need challenges to grow spiritually.

❧

Toward the end of his life, several of us were walking with Swami in his garden. At one point he stopped, and when he resumed walking, he told us that he had just recalled an expression on Yogananda's face that made him realize what Yogananda had meant by something he'd said sixty years earlier. Meditation stills the oscillating mirror of our minds. Attunement can come by reflecting on a master's every word, thought, and action until his true meaning finally reveals itself—even sixty years later!

❧

Swami was severely tested during a number of periods in his life. After one such period he took seclusion. Upon his return, he gave the Sunday service, and during the Festival of Light he was especially moved by the song "You Remain Our Friend." Barely able to speak, he asked that it be repeated a second time (as, back then, it was sung only once). After this experience, he edited the Festival so that we would sing it twice through. Listening sensitively to the words, it's possible to feel the depth of his experience:

> Long we feared to face Your love,
> Lest our emptiness it prove!
> Now at last our hearts we give You,
> Who remain our Friend.

❧

Swami was interested in the ideas of the architect Buckminster Fuller, who had designed buildings in the shape of a geodesic dome. Swami explained that the round roof of a dome mirrors the shape of the human head; thus instead of constricting our vibrations as squares or rectangles do, the dome allows our consciousness to energetically expand.

In the late 1970s, Swami lived in a rustic, unfinished dome that was part of the monastery, situated in a quiet area on the north side of the hill. A joke—but one based in reality—had it that the Native Americans knew better than to live on the shady north slope, where it was cold and dark and not much could grow. The dome was surrounded by tall forest and thick underbrush. Next to it, a small area had been cleared for an above-ground swimming pool where he would host pool parties with various groups of residents. At some of these gatherings, he declared that someday beautiful gardens would replace the forest on the hillside. Although it seemed impossible to imagine at the time—and that old joke notwithstanding—it came to pass exactly as he had predicted. Today, the setting is so beautiful that each year a growing number of visitors—18,000 of them in 2024—come to enjoy the tens of thousands of tulips set in gorgeously landscaped settings.

In time, Swami's dome gained—at last!—a new, watertight roof, and his home, now re-christened "Crystal Hermitage," expanded to include lovely public spaces with furnishings from around the world. Crystal Hermitage served as the community's spiritual hub. When he was at the original community, Swami lived there in a modest apartment on a lower level extending from the side of the main building. He described the Hermitage and his architectural ideals, and offered many interesting reflections on life and on his own life in particular, in a book he published: *Space, Light, and Harmony*.

Anyone who stands on those grounds or inside Crystal Hermitage today will experience the stunning beauty of the gardens, the dramatic views, and the peaceful vibrations.

❦

At the time, the taking down of the forest to create Crystal Hermitage with its surrounding gardens was controversial. It was hard to imagine the beauty which would take its place. Swami had no difficulty, of course, and I have often reflected that this was true also of how Swami viewed us: We saw only the "underbrush" when we looked in the mirror, but he saw our astral beauty. This is how God views us: as beautiful astral beings!

❦

In the construction of Crystal Hermitage—the building itself and its gardens—Swami was following in his guru's footsteps. Yogananda set a high aesthetic bar for landscaping and architecture, as is most readily apparent at the beautiful Lake Shrine in Los Angeles, and on the grounds of his Encinitas hermitage.

Yogananda took care to help people see God's light and smiles reflected in those buildings and gardens. Like music, the architecture of buildings and landscapes can touch the heart more deeply than words. For eight years it was my blessing to serve in offices on the Hermitage grounds, and each time I entered them, I would pinch myself to make sure I hadn't entered some higher astral realm.

Now that I live in the community in Washington State, I feel blessed whenever I enter the beautiful Blue Lotus Temple, which has the same design Swami chose for the temple in Assisi. Swami wanted our "official" architecture to reflect Yogananda's teachings and his vibrations. The grounds are beautifully landscaped, and it is easy to see God's smile, not only in the temple but also the flowers, and in the souls who come here for meditation, yoga, service, and fellowship. We call it the Blue Lotus Temple because it resembles the blue lotuses that Yogananda placed at the entrance to his Encinitas hermitage. Strangers often tell us how inspired they are by the beauty of the temple; it touches a universal chord.

※

During Swami's years in Yogananda's ashram, Yogananda gave him broad hints that he had a work for him to do in India. He made plans several years running to visit India and to bring Swami with him, plans, however, that had to be canceled each time, the last time on account of Yogananda's passing. Swami continued to ask in prayer whether his guru wanted him to pursue those hints; never, however, did he receive any guidance to do so.

Fast forward forty-five years after the Master's passing, to 1997. The publishing house that I directed for Swami had contracts with seven Indian publishers to put out a selection of Swami's books in India. Swami and I were repeatedly having the same conversation. He would ask me to contact those publishers (in the 1990s, "contacting" meant phoning them) to see if they would like to pay his way to India to offer lectures that would promote his books.

Books in India retail for significantly less than in the U.S.—a book that costs $10 in the U.S. might sell for as little as $2 in India.

Indian publishers thus weren't in the habit of paying for promotional tours. (Now, in 2024, even U.S. publishers rarely pay for an author to go on tour.) Still, I made the calls as he had requested. Each time, they would decline, and I would tell Swami.

Intuitively, I understood that these efforts were designed more to create a directional flow of energy than in any expectation of receiving an affirmative reply from the publishers. Swami had often told us that Babaji wanted Yogananda to be better known in India (and not only in the West). Swami was testing the waters, to see if Babaji was calling him to India. Now in his seventies, time was not his friend in this regard.

In 2003, an American couple unknown to Swami visited him at his home near the Assisi, Italy, community. Thoroughly disillusioned with Yogananda's organization in India, where they had long served as volunteers, they had resigned. That organization was hopelessly hidebound, they explained, and unsuited to making Yogananda widely known in the land of his birth.

Here—finally!—at the age of seventy-seven, was the guidance Swami had so long sought. He immediately gathered a small team and left for India, where he began founding ashrams dedicated to spreading Yogananda's teachings there.

The point here is that Swami was not passive, nor only prayerful, in his thoughts about India. He kept taking steps in that direction until God responded! Yogananda describes intuition as the soul's power to know God. Intuition is not passive: It requires action, that its validity be tested through our experience of the results.

❧

I once asked Swami for his thoughts on the tests that a certain person was undergoing. He offered some ideas that he felt would help the individual involved. Then I asked him how I could best convey those ideas. "Instead of 'counseling,' he suggested, "weave a pertinent point for him into a class or a talk at Sunday service, so that he can use his intuition to hear it." The universe can speak to us in this way through many voices. The wise person remains open and learns via intuitive understanding, not simply through words.

❧

To the ministers who gave talks at Sunday services, Swami suggested that they play at least one chant during the service, as it would help them become centered in the intuitive heart before their talk begins.

Yogananda used to say, "Chanting is half the battle." I have experienced that when I chant, no matter what it is that I go on to do that day, my heart is more open to learn the lessons that my activities can teach me. You might enjoy giving this a try yourself.

❧

Swami suggested that on the anniversary of Paramhansa Yogananda's final, conscious passing from his physical body—his *mahasamadhi*—we celebrate his life by focusing on the universality of his teachings, rather than on personality traits unique to him that, however charming they may be, could give the impression that what he brought was specific to him and to that particular incarnation.

In his autobiography, Yogananda writes of his visits to many different saints. In doing so, he entertains us with their colorful differences, but always in such a way as to emphasize the sameness of their essential teachings.

Masters, like the rest of us, must of necessity, in incarnating, "don" a personality. In Yogananda's case that personality was a remarkable one: Swami describes it at some length in a chapter in his book *Paramhansa Yogananda: A Biography*. And yet Master was far more than that superficial exterior. Swami, when telling us stories about Yogananda, would share vignettes revealing of his personality, so that we too could get a feeling of what it was like to live with him. And yet he did it in such a way as always to draw our attention to the universal mission and message that was his life's true purpose.

To prepare us for speaking in public, Swami encouraged us to avoid speaking in a monotone, and to end our sentences on a slightly raised pitch, or at least on a level pitch, but never dropping down. And for passages that were to be read, he encouraged us to practice reading them aloud at home, in order to absorb the meaning and thus find the right intonation for each sentence. Once I put this into practice, I found to my surprise that getting the intonation right opened a richer understanding of the meaning itself.

❧

Swami asked me to work with a new member he wanted to involve in one of his projects. He seemed to place a lot of trust in this person. After a few days, though, I felt I needed to let Swami know that his abilities were not what Swami thought they were. I had barely uttered two words when Swami said, "I know." The look in his eyes spoke volumes—they said, "No need to say anything further. I know. You can stay positive."

When we criticize or think negative thoughts about someone, even if our analysis is accurate, some of the negativity is bound to rub off on us in subtle ways. Through this example and many similar experiences, I learned to be more aware of my thoughts and words, and to do my best to frame others in a positive light, or else not speak at all.

❧

A few of us had come to the Assisi community from America to celebrate Swami's birthday, when we learned that the community's leaders wanted us all to speak at a morning program where Swami would not be present and tell stories of our experiences with him. When Swami heard about it, he was aghast. "Please, friends, only tell stories with a point: not what foods I like, and how I drink my coffee!"

We learned long ago to do the same for any public talks. Sri Yukteswar put it this way: Only tell stories (when appropriate) with a spiritual point, if possible, and even then, be sure to *articulate* the point!

❦

When Swami talked about Kriya Yoga, the highest technique of meditation on our path, he often said that he had set a minimum number of Kriyas that he would do in every meditation, and that he would never do fewer.

Swami suggested that everyone set his own minimum. Still, that was a recommendation, not a requirement. He never made a major point of these details; he left it to us to take what was meaningful for us personally. Yogananda's teachings are practiced from the inside out, not from outside in.

When we come from outside, the mind can play tricks on us. In this example, it might lead us to be too tough on ourselves, or too easy. Coming from the inside out, exercising our intuition when making decisions like this, helps our intuition become stronger.

If we err in the process of following our developing intuition, we will be guided to correct ourselves. God watches the heart, as Swami often reminded us, not the mind. If we're sincere, yet are doing too few Kriyas as our minimum, He will make it evident to us in time, as we will find it difficult to be silent or still.

❦

Sometimes, when people would wonder how something under consideration would play out in the future, Swami would quietly say, "Let's see how it evolves." His point was that we should base our spiritual lives on our own direct experience, rather than our mental projections. When he wrote the guidelines for the Monastic (Sevaka) Order, he remarked that he had waited almost twenty years to do it, until he could base those guidelines on the lived experiences of the community and its residents, on what had proved beneficial and what had not, rather than on some beautiful theory which might or might not have worked.

༄

Swami often said that the test of a spiritual idea should always be, "Does it work?" That was the gold standard: *Does it actually work?* Spirituality isn't a mere theory, or a mental construct: Our spirituality is tested, as Sister Gyanamata said, "in the cold light of day."

༄

Swami wrote a series of gift books called *Secrets*, each of them on a topic such as success, happiness, or meditation, and presenting a different "secret" for each day of the month. There were sixteen books for adults and four for children. A Danish publisher bought the rights for his language, and asked if Swami had any photographs he could use to illustrate each "secret."

The existing books had been illustrated with line drawings by community members. The publisher felt that Swami's nature photographs would make a more harmonious presentation: Since the author had taken the photographs, they would have the same vibration as the text. Swami was pleased at the publisher's perceptivity, and asked me to choose the photos. The books came out beautifully, and sold well. The publisher went on to translate and publish several of Swami's other books.

Swami led a gathering where people could submit written questions in advance. One question was overly intellectual and ended with, "Please don't tell me that the answer to this question is to love God." Swami responded strongly, saying that just because he, as a direct disciple of Paramhansa Yogananda, had written many books and lectured far and wide, it did not mean that people should necessarily follow in his footsteps. He felt that all of Yogananda's disciples should look to the way Yogananda had lived—and that Yogananda had always led with the heart. Therefore, the only answer *was* to love God. He cited, as an example of what he was not recommending, how the disciples of Ramakrishna ended up following the more philosophical way of Vivekananda, Ramakrishna's direct disciple, notwithstanding that the essence of Ramakrishna's life had been deeply devotional.

Swami explained that devotees should not get confused and miss the point of the vast reach of the Guru's teaching; they should tune in to his essence to guide them. In truth, love is always the essence of a fully liberated master. Jesus, for example, may have spoken in parables and shared great teachings through words that could sometimes be obscure, but the essence of his message was his twin commandments: "Love the Lord thy God with all thy heart, mind, soul, and strength," and ("like unto it") "Love thy neighbor as thyself."

What matters much more than what we do is the consciousness with which we do it. Swami could have pointed out that, like Yogananda, who also lectured and wrote extensively, he too always led with his heart, and no less so in his writings, as any sensitive reader can recognize. Swami responded to that man as he did because he saw that his focus on intellectual matters was reinforcing, to his detriment, an outlook that was already lacking in devotion.

Swami said: "The reason I write is to inspire people to *act*!" Yogananda came to offer people techniques and a way of life that could give them their own direct experience of God. Swami's effort was always to further Yogananda's purpose. He didn't write only to inspire people, but to inspire them *to take action in their spiritual lives*.

When a movie about Gandhi came out, Swami said, with tongue planted firmly in cheek, that the sequel would be called *The Empire Strikes Back* (a reference to a *Star Wars* movie). Like Yogananda, he had a delightful sense of humor.

Swami recommended that new ministers practice reading the Festival of Light aloud in their meditation room, so as to help them become deeply attuned to the vibration and meaning of each word. This practice is powerful for everyone. Swami published part of the Festival of Light toward the end of his book, *Cities of Light*. And you can find the entire Festival online at crystalclarity.com/271.

At a time when there were endless discussions among the community leaders about ways to "train" new ministers, I seem to recall that an outline was made and shown to Swami. His response was to put a stop to that way of thinking; it was too structured.

"The next thing you know," he said, "they will offer a diploma that says, 'Doctor of Delusion.'" This was a term Yogananda had coined for Christian ministers who were proud of their DD degrees (Doctor of Divinity). Yogananda encouraged everyone to think first of deepening his inner life and adopting an intuitive approach to spirituality. Each minister's journey will be hands on and unique in this regard.

Moreover, Swami often commented that a minister is one who, while in the midst of his own tests, thinks of the welfare of others. In other words, it is the minister's spirit, not his knowledge of the teachings, which qualifies him to be ordained a minister.

※

My husband and I were on vacation with Swami in Lugano, Switzerland. Swami loved that alpine city, with its beauty, artistry, delicious food, and chocolates. At one point, we entered a large department store that was famous for its fabulous cafeteria. When we passed a man demonstrating the latest type of nonstick frying pan, Swami stopped to watch, then purchased one and gave it to me as a gift. "You're a young mother," he said. "I'm sure you will appreciate this!"

I thanked him, though my husband and I had no idea how we would fit the pan into our suitcases while traveling around Europe and back to America.

Once home, I began to understand the wisdom of Swami's gift. I had to spend an enormous amount of time in the kitchen to feed our young family, and each time I used the pan I thought of Swami, and by extension, of Yogananda, and then of God. I'd had no idea that the pan would inspire me to practice God's presence, but Swami had known. I am glad that we persevered through the inconvenience of gallivanting all over Europe with a large frying pan! Attunement means listening within for God's voice, and not letting it be drowned out by the crosscurrents of the rational mind.

Paramhansa Yogananda told Swami to eat three meals per day. Swami never wavered. At home, or when traveling, no matter how large a previous meal had been, or how recent, he *always* ate three meals. He had promised his Guru that he would do so, and his word was his bond, even in the least of things.

When I began working on Swami's special projects, our children were four and six. Between my more-than-full-time job, a young family, and my meditation practice, there weren't enough hours in the day. At one point, Swami went into a writing seclusion to work on the rewriting of his book, *Crises in Modern Thought*.* He began sending me chapters to read so that I could offer him my feedback.

Aside from the fact that I had no time for reading, the subject of the book was not my forte. I prefer to read philosophy through stories and illustrations, rather than "straight up." Moreover, the book was intended for those who "want to believe, but don't know how." I *already did* believe, so I wasn't the intended audience.

Yet Swami kept sending me chapters, with notes that asked for my specific thoughts. Finally, I felt that I couldn't procrastinate any longer. I asked my husband if he could take the children for an outing the following Saturday and allow me a full day to read.

---

* Which he then republished under the title *Out of the Labyrinth: For Those Who Want to Believe, But Can't.*

He kindly agreed. I'm not a fast reader, but I completed about half of the book.

By that time, Swami had finished the first draft and had moved on to the editing phase. Now he asked me what I thought—again. This time, I wrote him a note describing my thoughts, with a few small edits. I tried to state my thoughts in such a way that he could imagine I had completed the book. The next day, I received a note thanking me for my thoughts on the first half of the book and asking what I thought of the second half. Never try to fool an intuitive soul!

༄

At one point while I managed the publishing department, Swami wrote, and we produced, a line of small gift books (the *Secrets* series mentioned above) that were wildly successful. There were twenty books in the series, and we sold them in picturesque displays. They were equally popular in book and gift stores. We received advance orders of more than fifty thousand copies each for most of the titles.

However, there was a catch. We had to be able to produce and print the books at one-tenth their retail price. No printers in the U.S. or Europe could meet that price. In the meantime, there was pressure from the sales team to get the books printed, lest we lose the orders, and Swami kept calling me to see when the printing would begin.

I was under pressure from all sides. Using Swami's own techniques of superconscious living, I persevered until I found a printer in Hong Kong who could come close to meeting the price we needed. I kept working with the man to lower the price by adjusting this or that feature, until we were able to meet the necessary cost per book. Sometimes being hemmed in by problems on all sides forces us to hold on to God's hem and seek our solutions from Him alone. Swami later commented that he appreciated my perseverance in seeking solutions, while honoring his guidance to get the books into print.

At one point I commented on a dynamic that was particularly challenging between two of the people in my department. Swami said, "I'm trying to delicately balance many energies right now." In other words, he was asking me to be patient, since there were many nuances of which I wasn't aware. It was a glimpse of the birds-eye view that God always has of us; things are not black and white, but there may be many shades of gray.

One year a beautiful event had been planned to celebrate Yogananda's mahasamadhi (his final conscious exit from the body). That morning, Swami called to say that he wasn't feeling well and wouldn't be able to attend. I told him I was sorry to hear the news, because he would miss this sacred opportunity to be close with his guru. Swami's calm response was, "I am always with him."

Yogananda was his constant touchstone in every second of his life. Swami's level of devotion and concentration is available to us all. It is the eternal divine promise for each and every soul: union with God through the guru is the essence of all spiritual paths.

༺

When each of our children was born, Swami came over within hours of the birth. Quietly, he made his way to the basinet and touched the baby in blessing at the point between the eyebrows (the spiritual eye). He had explained to us that this helps draw the life force to that point.

It is the entire purpose of Yogananda's meditation techniques and all yogic practices to draw the life force in time to the highest spiritual center, the crown chakra at the top of the head. Yogananda explained, however, that our task is to focus rather at the spiritual eye, for once that center is experienced clearly, the life force automatically makes its way to the crown chakra.

Swami was simply helping our babies along their way. What a blessing this was for them, and for the whole family.

༺

In the late 1980s, a dear friend at the original community contracted AIDS. At the time, medications for the deadly disease were in the early research stages, which meant that there wasn't much hope for her survival. She worked in my department, and when she confided her situation, I arranged for her to see Swami. He urged her to keep her heart and mind focused one-pointedly on Divine Mother in every moment that she possibly could. My friend embraced his advice and spent hours each day chanting. She didn't feel well, so meditation was difficult, but her heart was fully engaged in her chanting.

I realized that his advice addressed three things: 1. The best healing is not to focus on healing, but to focus on God alone. 2. With her heart and mind on God, she wasn't thinking about her illness, which would only have given the illness more energy, and 3. With her heart and mind on God, she was focused on her highest Self.

She fought the good fight for a number of years, then finally the disease took her body. But not her spirit: Her spirit soared!

Swami encouraged the leaders to go to the original community as often as possible. A few years after we had been living in Seattle, he had the idea for the leaders in Palo Alto, together with my husband and me, to purchase a modular "cottage on wheels" and place it in the lower garden of the Crystal Hermitage grounds (where the gazebo is now). In this way, we would be able to "come home" anytime we could get away, without having to scramble for housing. Though his idea didn't manifest, his message was clear: it was important for our attunement that we touch in at the original community as often as possible, and he was extending us an invitation to reside on the grounds as his neighbors.

❧

At times, I noticed that Swami would invite people to accompany him on trips that were unlikely to take place. Or he might say that he would like to visit them, yet I would know that this wasn't likely to occur. Even if they never happened, though, one felt from his having proposed them that he cared. And he was always sincere in what he said.

❧

Paramhansa Yogananda told his young disciple, Kriyananda, "Edit like lightning, but don't change a word." Contemplating this seemingly impossible instruction, Swami finally understood that Yogananda meant for him not to change a *thought*.

I witnessed a friend suggest to Swami an edit for several of the musical notes in one of Yogananda's more difficult chants. The high notes were challenging; thus it wasn't an arbitrary suggestion. But Swami declined to make the changes. Several years later, he did try the effect of altering a few of the notes, but some time after that, looking afresh at the change he'd introduced, he was surprised he'd even considered it. Swami would never edit his guru's works unless he felt a clear intuition from the Guru to do so.

Intuition and Attunement

When our children were young, a friend and prior resident of the original community (who was an astrologer) sent us the gift of astrological readings for each of us. Until then, I had hesitated to ask for readings, lest they interfere with developing my own intuition and decision-making.

During my reading, she said, "When your son enters high school, your form of service will change from working on projects to serving people ministerially." At the time of the reading, our son was perhaps three, and I completely forgot about her comments. Years later, though, when our son graduated from middle school, Swami asked our family to move to Seattle to serve as directors of the work there. Just days after he invited us to move, I remembered the reading and listened to it again. Amazingly, the timing was exact! When I mentioned this to Swami, he was as surprised as we were. He was simply acting on inner guidance, without any consideration of astrological factors. This didn't surprise me. These intuitive perceptions came to Swami endlessly, as a result of his deep attunement with the Divine Mother.

When our children were young, my husband and I took turns attending classes and Sunday services. Audio recordings had arrived on the scene, and Swami was pleased that all our programs were being recorded.

Once, I bumped into Swami the day after he had given a class. I commented that my husband had enjoyed the class, and that I was sorry I'd missed it. "Get the tape," he suggested. Some weeks later, when the same thing happened, he made the same comment, "Get the tape."

Well, I realized that I needed to get the tape! It wasn't enough to feel sad that I'd missed the class, or to compliment him because others had enjoyed it. My missing the class didn't mean that I had received a pass to neglect my spiritual growth that day. Attunement is *listening*! I needed to make the effort to listen to the tape and absorb the vibrations and teachings into my consciousness; no one else could do that for me.

༺༻

A devotee traveling with Swami in Italy asked, "Swami, when you are gone, what will we do without you?" Swami answered, "When I am gone, I will continue to serve Yogananda through you all."

Afterword

SWAMI SENT ME thousands of emails, faxes, and notes. Among them, I found the following email, which makes a poignant ending for this book. Swami would repeat to me, over and over, that I should train others so that I could move on to my next assignment. Most people cling to the known, but he encouraged me (and others) to reach for the unknown. In his note, it is apparent that he himself lived this truth unreservedly, ever ready to move forward without attachment. Swami wrote it to me and a few friends in the last few weeks of his life:

4/6/2013

Dear Ones:

Next month I will turn eighty-seven. I feel a need to disinvolve myself from many community decisions. It isn't that my mental clarity is diminishing. It's rather a growing feeling that I must redirect my activities. I just can't keep up with things enough to make responsible decisions anymore. Too many details to be aware of. I just don't care to remain that involved. Do you understand? What is involving me now is the movies I feel I must do.

Please help me with this process. You are all very competent. I have built this work consciously with the thought of gradually passing the management of it to others.

A study was made years ago of organizations after the death of their founders. In nearly every case, the organizations failed. In the few that continued to exist, drastic changes occurred. One [counter]example comes to my mind: Walt Disney. I have always tried to develop things in such a way that they would continue to thrive in the same spirit once I was off the scene.

Please, let's think now about the future. Eighty-seven may not indicate the end of my life, but surely it presages the approaching end. And I have to add that I've never done anything with the thought that it belonged to me. It isn't yours, either. It belongs to Master and God.

With love, your brother,

nayaswami kriyananda

[ABOVE] Nayaswami Padma, Swami Kriyananda, and Nayaswami Hriman, Seattle, WA, 2000.
[BELOW] Standing before Mt. Etna, in Taormina, Italy, 2001.

About the Author

NAYASWAMI PADMA MCGILLOWAY is a disciple of Paramhansa Yogananda through his direct disciple, Swami Kriyananda, whom she met at the age of nineteen in 1970. Her leadership and teaching skills were honed over her forty-three years as his student and friend, until his passing in 2013. During those years living in the spiritual cooperative communities he had founded, she served him closely in a succession of leadership positions, and learned from him also through thousands of opportunities to enjoy his company in more informal settings.

Padma and her husband Hriman joined the original community in California in the 1970s, where they raised their two children. They led retreats, taught classes, and were ministers and counselors as well as leaders in various aspects of Swami Kriyananda's work throughout those years.

During the period when Swami Kriyananda published many of his 150 books, Padma was the head of his publishing house, Crystal Clarity, Publishers. For some twenty-six years she represented him at the annual publishing trade show in Frankfurt,

Germany, through which his books have been published in over fifty languages.

In 1993 Padma and Hriman accepted Kriyananda's invitation to become the co-spiritual directors of the community in Seattle that he'd founded. They continue to live and serve there, offering classes and spiritual counseling to help people go deeper in their spiritual lives. And as a Kriyacharya (one who initiates people into Kriya meditation practice), ordained by Swami Kriyananda, she has developed and directed highly successful training programs in this highest technique of spiritual liberation that Yogananda taught, one that he described as the "jet airplane" path to God.

Further Explorations

CRYSTAL CLARITY PUBLISHERS

If you enjoyed this title, Crystal Clarity Publishers invites you to deepen your spiritual life through many additional resources based on the teachings of Paramhansa Yogananda. We offer books, e-books, audiobooks, yoga and meditation videos, and a wide variety of inspirational and relaxation music composed by Swami Kriyananda.

See a listing of books below, visit our secure website for a complete on-line catalog, or place an order for our products.

crystalclarity.com
800.424.1055 | clarity@crystalclarity.com
14618 Tyler Foote Rd. | Nevada City, CA 95959

ANANDA WORLDWIDE

Crystal Clarity Publishers is the publishing house of Ananda, a worldwide spiritual movement founded by Swami Kriyananda, a direct disciple of Paramhansa Yogananda. Ananda offers resources and support for your spiritual journey through meditation instruction, webinars, online virtual community, email, and chat.

Ananda has more than 150 centers and meditation groups in over 45 countries, offering group guided meditations, classes and teacher training in meditation and yoga, and many other resources.

In addition, Ananda has developed eight residential communities in the US, Europe, and India. Spiritual communities are places where people live together in a spirit of cooperation and friendship, dedicated to a common goal. Spirituality is practiced in all areas of daily life: at school, at work, or in the home. Many Ananda communities offer internships during which one can stay and experience spiritual community firsthand.

For more information about Ananda communities or meditation groups near you, please visit ananda.org or call 530.478.7560.

THE EXPANDING LIGHT RETREAT

The Expanding Light is the largest retreat center in the world to share exclusively the teachings of Paramhansa Yogananda. Situated in the Ananda Village community near Nevada City, California, the center offers the opportunity to experience spiritual life in a contemporary ashram setting. The varied, year-round schedule of classes and programs on yoga, meditation, and spiritual practice includes Karma Yoga, personal retreat, spiritual travel, and online learning. Large groups are welcome.

The Ananda School of Yoga & Meditation offers certified yoga, yoga therapist, spiritual counselor, and meditation teacher trainings.

The teaching staff has years of experience practicing Kriya Yoga meditation and all aspects of Paramhansa Yogananda's teachings. You may come for a relaxed personal renewal, participating in ongoing activities as much or as little as you wish. The serene mountain setting, supportive staff, and delicious vegetarian meals provide an ideal environment for a truly meaningful stay, be it a brief respite or an extended spiritual vacation.

For more information, please visit expandinglight.org or call 800.346.5350.

ANANDA MEDITATION RETREAT

Set amidst seventy-two acres of beautiful meditation gardens and wild forest in Northern California's Sierra foothills, the Ananda Meditation Retreat is an ideal setting for a rejuvenating, inner experience.

The Meditation Retreat has been a place of deep meditation and sincere devotion for over fifty years. Long before that, the Native American Maidu tribe held this to be sacred land. The beauty and presence of the Divine are tangibly felt by all who visit here.

Studies show that being in nature and using techniques such as forest bathing can significantly reduce stress and blood pressure while strengthening your immune system, concentration, and level of happiness. The Meditation Retreat is the perfect place for quiet immersion in nature.

Plan a personal retreat, enjoy one of the guided retreats, or choose from a variety of programs led by the caring and joyful staff.

For more information or to make your reservation, please visit meditationretreat.org, email meditationretreat@ananda.org, or call 530.478.7557.

THE ORIGINAL 1946 UNEDITED EDITION
OF YOGANANDA'S SPIRITUAL MASTERPIECE

AUTOBIOGRAPHY OF A YOGI
Paramhansa Yogananda

Autobiography of a Yogi is one of the world's most acclaimed spiritual classics, with millions of copies sold. Named one of the Best 100 Spiritual Books of the twentieth century, this book helped launch and continues to inspire a spiritual awakening throughout the Western world.

Yogananda was the first yoga master of India whose mission brought him to settle and teach in the West. His firsthand account of his life experiences in India includes childhood revelations, stories of his visits to saints and masters, and long-secret teachings of yoga and Self-realization that he first made available to the Western reader.

This reprint of the original 1946 edition is free from textual changes made after Yogananda's passing in 1952. This updated edition includes bonus materials: the last chapter that Yogananda wrote in 1951, also without posthumous changes, the eulogy Yogananda wrote for Gandhi, and a new foreword and afterword by Swami Kriyananda, one of Yogananda's close, direct disciples.

Also available in Spanish and Hindi from Crystal Clarity Publishers.

PARAMHANSA YOGANANDA
A Biography with Personal Reflections and Reminiscences
Swami Kriyananda

Paramhansa Yogananda's life was filled with astonishing accomplishments. And yet in his classic autobiography, he wrote more about the saints he'd met than about his own spiritual attainments. Yogananda's direct disciple, Swami Kriyananda, relates the untold story of this great master and world teacher: his teenage miracles, his challenges in coming to America, his national lecture campaigns, his struggles to fulfill his world-changing mission amid incomprehension and painful betrayals, and his ultimate triumphant achievement.

Kriyananda's subtle grasp of his guru's inner nature and outward mission reveals Yogananda's many-sided greatness. Includes many never-before-published anecdotes and an insider's view of the Master's last years.

THE NEW PATH
My Life with Paramhansa Yogananda
Swami Kriyananda

Winner of the 2010 Eric Hoffer Award for Best Self-Help/Spiritual Book
Winner of the 2010 USA Book News Award for Best Spiritual Book

The New Path is a moving revelation of one man's search for lasting happiness. After rejecting the false promises offered by modern society, J. Donald Walters found himself (much to his surprise) at the feet of Paramhansa Yogananda, asking to become his disciple. How he got there, trained with the Master, and became Swami Kriyananda makes fascinating reading.

The rest of the book is the fullest account by far of what it was like to live with and be a disciple of that great man of God.

Anyone hungering to learn more about Yogananda will delight in the hundreds of stories of life with a great avatar and the profound lessons they offer. This book is an ideal complement to *Autobiography of a Yogi*.

THE NEED FOR SPIRITUAL COMMUNITIES AND HOW TO START THEM
Swami Kriyananda

In this book Swami Kriyananda shares the wisdom gained through many decades of study and practice of the principles that make modern communities thrive. Inspired by his guru, Paramhansa Yogananda, and his ideal of "world brotherhood colonies," Kriyananda brought these principles to fruition through persistent effort and inspired leadership.

Kriyananda (1926–2013) founded nine spiritual communities in the United States, Europe, and India that have been hailed as among the most successful in the world. They are based on two fundamental tenets: "People are more important than things" and "Where there is right action, there is victory." Adherence to these principles is one of the secrets to Ananda's success.

Whether you are interested in communities from a philosophical perspective or from a practical one—and wish to form your own or join with others in doing so—this book will bring you hundreds of helpful insights into the process: how to start a community, how to make it prosper even in difficult times, and how to see it continue into a bright future.

CONVERSATIONS WITH YOGANANDA
Stories, Sayings, and Wisdom of Paramhansa Yogananda
Recorded with reflections, by his disciple, Swami Kriyananda

For those who enjoyed Paramhansa Yogananda's autobiography and long for more, this collection of conversations offers rare intimate glimpses of life with the Master as never before shared.

This is an unparalleled account of Yogananda and his teachings written by one of his foremost disciples. Swami Kriyananda was often present when Yogananda spoke privately with other close disciples, received visitors and answered their questions, and dictated and discussed his writings. He recorded the Master's words, preserving a treasure trove of wisdom that would otherwise have been lost.

These Conversations include not only Yogananda's words as he spoke them, but the added insight of a disciple who spent over fifty years attuning his consciousness to that of his guru.

The collection features nearly five hundred stories, sayings, and insights from the twentieth century's most famous master of yoga, as well as twenty-five photos—nearly all previously unreleased.

THE ESSENCE OF SELF-REALIZATION
The Wisdom of Paramhansa Yogananda
Paramhanda Yogananda
Edited by his disciple, Swami Kriyananda

Filled with lessons, stories, and jewels of wisdom that Paramhansa Yogananda shared only with his closest disciples, this volume is an invaluable guide to the spiritual life, carefully organized in twenty main topics.

Great teachers work through their students, and Yogananda was no exception. Swami Kriyananda comments, "After I'd been with him a year and a half, he began urging me to write down the things he was saying during informal conversations." Many of the three hundred sayings presented here are available nowhere else. This book and *Conversations with Yogananda* are must-reads for anyone wishing to know more about Yogananda's teachings and to absorb his wisdom.

For more titles in books, audiobooks, spoken word, music, and videos, and for a complete online catalog of Crystal Clarity Publishers products, visit crystalclarity.com.

www.ingramcontent.com/pod-product-compliance
Lightning Source LLC
Chambersburg PA
CBHW071710090426
42738CB00009B/1735